The Spirit and the Sword

a western way of swordsmanship

The Spirit and the Sword

a western way of swordsmanship

John Michael Greer

New Hermetics Press
Sarasota, FL

First published in 2008 by
The New Hermetics Press
P. O. Box 18111
Sarasota, FL 34276
www.newhermetics.com
www.newhermeticspress.com

Copyright © 2008 John Michael Greer

All rights reserved. No part of this publication may be reproduced or transmitted in any form or by any means, electronic or mechanical, including photocopying, recording, or by any information storage and retrieval system, without permission in writing from The New Hermetics Press. Reviewers may quote brief passages.

ISBN: 978-0-578-01309-1

Cover Design, interior art and typesetting by Fr∴ E. I. A. E.

15 14 13 12 11 10 09 08
8 7 6 5 4 3 2 1

Acknowledgments

Neither the discovery of the material central to this book, nor the creation of the book itself, would have been possible without the help of many other people. Some of them, for a variety of reasons, must be nameless here, and it has also seemed best not to name the order which originally provided me with the legacy of sword teachings that made this project possible. My debt to the individuals in question, and to the order to which they have given so much, is immense, and must be acknowledged here.

At the top of the list of those whom I can thank by name belongs my wife Sara, whose love and practical support have been essential in this, as in all my projects. Special thanks are also due to Carl Hood Jr., Darren Lay, and Jeff Richardson, each of whom provided important assistance along the way. Also deserving of thanks are the staff of the Seattle Public Library interlibrary loan department, who time and again found me the sources I needed to follow up on my first discoveries and expand them into a practical Western way of the sword. My gratitude remains with all.

Table of Contents

Chapter One: A Western Way of Swordsmanship   9

Chapter Two: Fundamentals of Sword Training   23

Chapter Three: Preparatory Exercises   41

Chapter Four: Relaxation and Breathing Exercises   59

Chapter Five: Footwork Training   71

Chapter Six: The Manual of the Sword   86

Chapter Seven: Attack and Defense   112

Chapter Eight: Free Practice   125

Chapter Nine: Additional Training Methods   133

Chapter Ten: Sword and Spear   144

Bibliography   167

Index   169

Chapter One
a western way of swordsmanship

Martial arts are not an exclusively Oriental phenomenon. Fighting methods of one type or another, armed or unarmed, are as old as humankind, and there have been plenty of cultures—all over the world and throughout history—where methods of combat have developed enough sophistication and subtlety to deserve the title "martial art."

The Western world is no exception to this rule. Until the early part of the twentieth century, in fact, several living Western martial arts were still practiced in European countries and in North America. This book is an instructional manual of one of these arts, a system of swordsmanship that flourished in the eighteenth and nineteenth centuries and was preserved, as a traditional practice in certain lodges, well into the twentieth.

Like many of the martial arts of the East, the tradition in question has certain connections to the realm of spirituality, and to subtle disciplines of consciousness and energy that make this art a fusion of the spirit and the sword. Historical and cultural differences between East and West have had an important impact on the way these connections have played out, though. In most of the ancient cultures of the Orient, spiritual disciplines and teachings of this sort have been taught openly for many centuries, and their practitioners hold positions of respect in the traditional social order.

In the West, matters were otherwise. A complex series of historical factors led the dominant religion of the Western world, Christianity, to prohibit such teachings and persecute those who followed them. Even after the Christian church lost its grip on the levers of political power, the scientific ideology that replaced it adopted many of its prejudices; the founders and propagandists of the Scientific Revolution rejected such "superstitious" perspectives and practices with no less zeal than their religious opponents—although their methods of repression were normally a good deal less brutal.

As a consequence, many of the inner traditions of the Western world survived for centuries in a cultural underground of occultism and spiritual dissent, where lodges and other little-known organizations bound to secrecy have preserved an extraordinary wealth of lore and practice. Since the dawn of the modern occult renaissance, one of the central challenges to students and scholars of the Western inner traditions has been to make use of this legacy, to recognize its potentials, and to piece together the often fragmentary material and restore it to some semblance of its original form.

The martial art covered in this book is one part of this legacy, and its recovery and reconstruction is part of my contribution to the broader project of renewing the heritage of the inner traditions of the West. The material explored here survived in at least one lodge organization until quite recent times. It was never subject to the oaths of secrecy that put so many details of lodge practice out of the reach of the uninitiated. What kept it out of the public eye was simply the utter lack of interest, on the part of two generations of Americans, in the entire world of lodge organizations and in their brilliant but forgotten cultural heritage.

The traditions of lodge practice have had an impact of their own on this material. Like much of what went on (and still goes on) behind lodge doors, the tradition of swordsmanship taught in this book was passed on through written instructions followed up by personal practice, rather than through the sort of master-pupil relationship so common in the martial arts of other cultures. This approach places some limits on what can be taught; the art of swordsmanship presented in these pages is a relatively basic one, and it needs to be filled out and brought to perfection by the pupil's own experiences with the sword, by relentless practice of the fundamental exercises, and by sparring with a wide range of partners.

At the same time, a martial art designed to be communicated by written words and pictures can be brought back to life long after the living tradition of practice has become extinct. It also fits the approach of an instructional manual like this one far better than those arts that require personal instruction from a master. While it's true that no martial art can be learned just by reading a book, my experience has been that this one can be learned, and mastered, by combining careful and systematic reading with intensive practice of the sequence of solo and paired training exercises that are central to the tradition, and with regular sparring practice with a variety of training partners. Indeed, it was in this way that the art was learned and mastered when it was in full flower a century ago.

Western Martial Ways

The art of swordsmanship passed on through these ways, and presented in this book, has its roots in a long history. A glance back through that history will provide some useful perspectives to the student. With apologies to those readers who would prefer to get right down to swordplay, then, we'll take a few moments here to glance back over the history of the martial arts in the West.

We know little about the oldest martial arts in the Western world—that is, those parts of the Old World centered on Europe and the Mediterranean Sea, where the cultures of most modern industrialized societies have their roots. By the fifth century before the Common Era, certainly, the warring city-states of ancient Greece had developed armed and unarmed combat to a high degree of skill. The Olympic games of those times included contests of wrestling, boxing, and pankration—a brutal, no-holds-barred unarmed combat sport in which contestants routinely died. Later, in the heyday of the Roman Empire, gladiators trained with wooden swords and evolved exotic weapons arts—for example, the retiarius, one class of gladiator, went into combat armed with a three-pronged spear and a circular net edged with lead weights.

These martial arts of the ancient world, complex and richly developed as they were, had little influence on the later development of combat methods in the West. North of the Empire, in the lands ruled by Celtic and Germanic tribes, the future of Western martial arts (and of the Western world) was already being born. As political corruption and civil war bled the Roman world dry, these warlike tribal peoples drove against the frontiers with growing strength, and their forays into the empire grew steadily harder to contain. When the frontier defenses shattered once and for all, in the fifth century of the Common Era, most of the empire fell quickly into the hands of tribal kings and warlords, and the Middle Ages dawned.

Racked with internal warfare and threatened by powerful forces from abroad—Muslim armies from the south, nomadic tribes such as the Magyars from the eastern steppes, and Viking raiders from the north—the new nations of Europe faced a fight for survival against heavy odds. The tribal societies that had defeated Rome were themselves shattered and reshaped by the demands of constant warfare. The new civilization of feudal Europe came into being, ruled by a warrior aristocracy, under the spiritual sway of an increasingly militant Christian church.

New technologies and tactics both fed and followed these sweeping social changes. While many of the tribal peoples that overwhelmed Rome fought on foot, the feudal aristocracy went to war on horseback, clad in armor from head to heel. Weapons changed little—the only major differences between a spatha of late Roman times and a sword from the high Middle Ages a thousand years later are the quality of the steel and the details of decoration—but methods of using them became ever more sophisticated in the endless feudal struggles for survival and supremacy.

Rigorous training prepared the knight for the extreme demands of hand-to-hand combat in heavy armor, and tournaments gave him the opportunity to test his skill in times of peace. The tournaments of the Middle Ages were much more serious than most modern people think, and involved much more than jousting—that is, combat with lances from horseback. Every kind of armed combat between individuals took place, along with full-scale pitched battles fought with blunted weapons. Broken bones were routine, and deaths far from rare.

It's in the high Middle Ages that we find the first solid documentary evidence of European martial arts. A few medieval manuscripts from the late thirteenth and early fourteenth centuries reveal the methods of knightly combat in some detail. Those who think of medieval warriors as muscular oafs swinging their weapons half at random have neglected their homework; these manuscripts describe canny and thoroughly developed systems of armed combat that can stand comparison with any martial art in the world. Techniques for sword, longsword, sword and buckler, lance, battleax, and other weapons were studied and practiced, along with techniques for fighting without weapons.

These arts, despite the stereotypes, were never under the exclusive control of the warrior aristocracy. Even the rural peasantry had its own martial arts—quarterstaff, bow, and a variety of polearms were among the common weapons in use among the lower classes, and wrestling and boxing were also much practiced. In the larger cities, where the power of the feudal nobility was weaker, commoners took up the study of combat arts early on, and fencing schools and fighting guilds appear in the historical records beginning in the twelfth century.

Among the Marxbrüder—the Brotherhood of the Golden Lion of St. Mark, the oldest of the German fighting guilds—the standard course of study included fencing with several different kinds of swords and pole arms, as well as a sophisticated system of wrestling. Similar rules governed the Schools of Defence in England, which existed in London by 1180. Competitions sponsored by these bodies were public events with large audiences, and those who aspired to the status of master faced stringent examinations before a committee of masters.

By the time the Marxbrüder and similar organizations were well established, gunpowder had already been introduced to Europe from China, and the first crude cannon and handguns were evolving step by step into weapons that would transform not only the battlefield, but society as a whole. The lifelong martial discipline and expensive armor of the medieval knight offered little protection against a musket in the hands of a peasant with two weeks' training. The feudal system began to crack as armies of pikemen and musketeers came to dominate the battlefield.

Paradoxically, these currents of change led, not to the demise of the martial arts of the West, but to their explosive spread and reformulation. Powerful as the new military technologies were on the battlefield, they were of little use in ordinary self-defense; reliable handguns were not even on the drawing boards for several more centuries. At the same time, the duel replaced the tournament as a way for aristocrats to settle their differences with steel. New ways of combat came into being; armor and shields were discarded, along with most of the panoply of medieval weaponry, and swordsmen of the new era learned to use their blades for defense as well as offense.

As technological change progressed and society adapted, these new fighting methods changed as well. Two major patterns dominated in this process. On the one hand, duelling swords and methods took on ever more specialized forms, responding to the artificial environment of the duelling field, and eventually gave

Chapter 1 – A Western Way of Swordsmanship

rise to modern fencing—a sport, pure and simple, with little connection to the realities of combat. The same process, later on, stripped Western boxing and wrestling of their combat effectiveness and turned them into sports as well.

On the other hand, the most practical aspects of the new swordsmanship worked their way back into a military context. The sword was still the weapon of the officer and the gentleman, and in an age when officers stood beside the men they commanded on the battlefield, skill with a sword still counted for something when the last volley of bullets rang out and the time came to fix bayonets and charge. Cavalry, too, still played an important role in war, and most types of cavalry still carried the sword as their primary weapon. Detailed systems of military swordsmanship thus came into being, and were publicized and described in a flourishing literature of sword manuals. These also interfaced with the popular genre of self-defense manuals during the same period, with a great deal of overlap between sword techniques and those of the walking stick or cane, a common self-defense weapon of the time.

These systems were still very much in use in the nineteenth century, and saw a final burst of development in the aftermath of the Napoleonic Wars in Europe and the Civil War in America. At the beginning of the twentieth century, the army of every major Western power had its corps of cavalry, armed with swords and lances, ready to reenact the victories of the past. Then came the First World War, and all the assumptions of generations of military theorists went down under machine-gun fire in the mud and trenches of the Western Front. The world had changed, and swordsmanship dropped from the training curriculum of most of the world's armies.

In the aftermath of the First World War, additionally, popular revulsion against modern warfare led to a widespread rejection of anything that seemed to relate to militarism or war, and the few surviving Western martial arts were easy targets. It's indicative that the Boy Scouts, which had revived the old English martial art of quarterstaff fighting before the war, quietly dropped it in 1919. By the time the martial arts of Asia began to attract significant interest in the West, in the aftermath of the American occupation of Japan in the late 1940s, very few people remembered that the Western world had still had martial arts of its own less than half a century before.

The Spiritual Dimension

Another dimension of the martial arts needs to be discussed at this point. Many of the martial arts of the Orient have profound connections to traditions of spiritual development, in which the demands of combat are met by way of methods drawing on the subtler powers of the human body and mind. It's impossible, for example, to separate t'ai chi ch'uan from its roots in Taoist philosophy and meditative practice, or to draw firm boundaries between Shaolin kung fu and the Buddhist teachings and traditions from which it arose. Similar links connect ninjutsu to esoteric Buddhism, aikido to certain little-known offshoots of Shinto, the Indian fighting art of kalarippayat to yoga and Hindu philosophy, and so on. To many people, it's the existence of such connections that raises a true martial art out of the realm of mere techniques of violence, and makes possible the unity of the spirit and the sword.

It's often been assumed that such connections are something unique to the cultures of east Asia, or to the specific religious and mystical traditions that fostered so rich a panoply of martial traditions in the Orient. Like martial arts themselves, however, warrior traditions with a spiritual and mystical dimension were far from rare in the Western world, and can be traced back to very early times.

Surviving fragments of the lore of the pagan Celtic and Germanic tribes, incomplete as they are, still make it clear that a range of inner disciplines of awareness and energy were practiced by warriors before the fall of Rome. Irish legends describe a battle-frenzy invoked by shamanic means, which made the warrior who used it immune to pain and shock, while amplifying his strength to terrifying levels. Similar accounts appear in the lore of

Chapter 1 – A Western Way of Swordsmanship

the Norse berserkr (literally, "bear-shirt") and ulfhednar ("wolf-warrior"), who gained similar powers through spiritual disciplines that are little understood today. While these powers are often dismissed as mythical, similar feats are still performed by shamans of many tribal cultures in a less violent context, and modern scholarship has begun to explore the shamanic roots of these and other warrior traditions of the past.

How much of this survived the transition from paganism to Christianity is anybody's guess. Recent scholarship has shown that an astonishing amount of pagan magic and spirituality was lightly Christianized and accepted into medieval culture, sometimes even with the knowledge and approval of the Church. The same attitude that led missionaries to convert pagan temples into Christian churches and pagan gods into Christian saints transformed a good deal of pagan magic into Christian ritual. Unfortunately, we know very little about the training and techniques of the warriors of the early Middle Ages, and so the survival of the old warrior arts of the tribal period is an open question. The tendency for theologically questionable practices to go on in secret, a pattern well attested in medieval Europe and elsewhere, adds a further source of confusion.

The history of the Middle Ages is full of such riddles, especially where the martial and the magical intertwine. The greatest of these puzzles involves the Order of Poor Knights of the Temple of Solomon, better known as the Knights Templar, a brotherhood of warrior monks founded in 1118 in the aftermath of the First Crusade. Starting out as a small band of knights pledged to defend pilgrims on the roads of the Holy Land, the Templars grew to become one of the largest and most powerful religious orders in the Western world, with castles throughout the Crusader kingdoms of Palestine and holdings all over Europe.

Their wealth and power, however, did not protect them forever. On a single day in 1307, in an operation reminiscent of modern police state tactics, every Templar brother in France was seized by officers of the French king Philip IV on charges of heresy. Most other European countries followed suit. The order was disbanded by order of the Pope, its properties seized, and some of its members—including the last Grand Master, Jacques de Molay—were burned at the stake.

Rumors linking the Templars with strange religious doctrines and practices were widely circulated at the time of their downfall. More recently, a good many of the same stories have been dusted off and enriched by new material, and a small-scale furore in the alternative press has grown up about the question of the Templars' real beliefs and purposes. Popular opinion at the time of the order's suppression, and the consensus of modern historians, is that the charges of heresy were a smokescreen covering the French king's greed for the Templars' treasure and real estate holdings. Whether this is true, or whether something else lies behind all the smoke, is anyone's guess at this point. Still, whatever the Templars' actual religious beliefs and practices, they combined the roles of monk and warrior just as much as any Shaolin priest or Taoist master. It's at least possible that they found ways to unite their spiritual disciplines with their combat training, reshaping the chivalric martial disciplines into something with a further dimension of meaning and power. If they did, however, no trace of the resulting art seems to have survived. More than two hundred years of research, ranging from the sensible to the wildly speculative, has failed to turn up anything. The suggestion remains, tantalizing but impossible to prove.

Within a century of the Templars' fall, though, the Middle Ages were crumbling and the Renaissance had dawned. Mystical, magical and philosophical traditions blossomed, and the inner traditions of the West took on forms that are still recognizable today. Martial arts with an openly revealed inner dimension were a logical outcome of this new freedom, and at least one found its way into the clear light of history during this time.

This was the Spanish style of rapier fencing, an elaborate tradition of swordsmanship that emerged sometime before 1582, and is still practiced and taught by a handful of people today. The rapier was a highly specialized duelling sword, long and slender, and it was the first great Spanish master of the rapier—the celebrated Jeronimo Carranza—who saw that it could be wielded in patterns drawn from the mystical lore of sacred geometry.

In the works of Carranza, of his great pupil Luis Pacheco de Narvaez, and of Gerard Thibault, who communicated the secrets of the Spanish style in the most elaborate fencing manual of all time, the traditions of sacred geometry and of Renaissance esoteric philosophy form the framework on which an effective combat art was created. Thibault's treatise, published in the Netherlands where restrictions on the press were minimal, goes so far as to quote major contemporary works of magical philosophy in its introductory chapter. The Spanish authors had to be more careful—the Inquisition was a fact of life in Spain at that time—but the same occult factors can be traced in subtler form in their writings as well.

Though modern historians of fencing tend to dismiss the Spanish style, contemporary writings make it clear that Spanish fencers had a continent-wide reputation as lethal duelists. Modern students of the sword who have put these methods to the test have also found them to be extraordinarily effective against other rapier styles—though rapier fencing methods do poorly against most other weapons. Complicated, demanding, and highly specialized, the Spanish style of swordsmanship still represents the Western world's best attempt so far to unite the spirit and the sword.

The end of the Renaissance and the coming of the Scientific Revolution brought a close to an era when alternative spiritual philosophies and practices could be openly taught and discussed in much of the Western world. Ridicule and official condemnation replaced torture and the stake, but the barriers to a free exploration of human potential were still very much back in place. In response, many followers of such traditions withdrew into lodges and similar semi-secret organizations, where they could preserve their traditions and practices in private, and stayed there until the cultural explosion of the Sixties brought magic and esoteric spirituality back out of the lodges and into the streets.

Habits of secrecy so long preserved make it very hard for the historian to track the development of any part of this elusive history, and the genesis of the specific method of swordsmanship discussed here is hidden in the resulting obscurity. All that can be said for certain is that at some point between 1870 and 1918, at least one lodge organization with links to the Western inner traditions either devised or adopted from elsewhere the system of swordsmanship taught in this book.

That system, in its practical aspect, has very extensive similarities with the standard military sword techniques taught in the late nineteenth century, while its inner aspect has much in common with other systems of personal development—especially the physical culture movement, another neglected treasure of our Western heritage with substantial links to esoteric spirituality—that were in circulation during those same years. None of this is particularly surprising, since occultists are people of their own place and time, and take in ideas and information from their surroundings like everyone else.

I have used both these sources, the manuals of swordsmanship and the handbooks of physical culture, to fill out the very fragmentary material that originally came into my hands. Readers who take the time to locate the books listed in the bibliography will be able to judge for themselves the extent to which my reconstruction of the original tradition draws on the systems of practical swordsmanship and inner development that were current in the early twentieth century, when the documents I received were apparently put together. Readers who take the time to learn and practice the techniques given here, on the other hand, will be able to judge for themselves whether the material I've given is worthwhile here and now—which is a very different matter.

The Relevance of Swordsmanship

It may not be out of place here to talk about why any system of swordsmanship is worthwhile in the modern age, and why people who have many other calls on their time might want to devote part of each day to learning a skill that seems so utterly outdated. The example of the Oriental martial arts, which use some weapons that are at least as archaic, shows that a good many people do want to put part of their time into such things—but why?

An important part of the answer lies in the spiritual dimension discussed above. Since ancient times warriors and mystics alike have been noticing that the demands of martial arts training and the requirements of the spiritual path are surprisingly similar. Both take courage and a willingness to face the unknown as fundamental requirements; both bring the self face to face with its own weaknesses and bad habits; both call for clarity, patience, self-discipline, a sense of humor, and an enormous amount of hard work. The development of inner, spiritual martial arts deepen these connections even further, since techniques using subtle energies or the less obvious powers of the mind can't be used at all without the sort of spiritual training that monks, mystics, and magicians use for their own purposes.

The result of these connections, in the case of the inner martial arts, is to remove any separation between martial training and spiritual practice, to create a perfect unity between the spirit and the sword. It's for this reason, in many cases, that people take up martial arts today. It is certainly a valid reason for taking up the martial art taught in this book, which has substantial interconnections with Western traditions of magic and esoteric spirituality, and can be combined with nearly any of the Western inner traditions harmoniously.

Other people study martial arts as methods for developing coordination and physical grace, developing strength, or simply taking in a healthy amount of exercise. All these are valid reasons for martial arts practice—and they are all valid reasons for the practice of this martial art. Leaving aside the spiritual dimensions of the system of swordsmanship taught here, it can be also be used simply as a form of physical conditioning or healthy exercise. (In fact, some parts of the tradition are aimed directly at these last two goals, since it takes a certain degree of coordination, grace, and strength to handle a sword effectively in the first place. Chapters 3 and 4 cover the key material here.)

Beyond the spiritual and health dimensions of the martial arts in general, of course, they also have a practical dimension as methods of self-protection, and so it may be worth adding a few words on the self-defense possibilities of the system discussed here. For a variety of reasons, I have not discussed the self-defense applications of swordsmanship in any detail, but they certainly exist. While a sword is hardly an appropriate weapon to carry on the streets of a modern city, the nineteenth- century sword manuals frequently comment that any technique that can be done with a sword can also be done with a walking stick. An ordinary walking stick made of any sturdy hardwood, three feet long and approximately an inch in diameter, is an effective self-defense tool that (as of this writing) is still legal to carry in all US jurisdictions.

With these matters of history and theory out of the way, then, it's time to turn from the past to the present—from the history of Western swordsmanship to the possibility of its present-day revival and practice. Our society, fascinated by modern technologies of mass carnage, laid down the sword nearly a century ago. Do you seek to take it up again? Read on.

Chapter Two
fundamentals of sword training

In this chapter we turn from the perspectives of history to the actual details of sword training. For most people nowadays, this is a venture onto very unfamiliar ground. Making sense of the old sword traditions means, for the modern student, covering a good deal of material that was common knowledge (or even common sense) to our ancestors. A hundred years ago, for example, most people in the Western world knew the names of the different parts of a sword; these days, by contrast, sword nomenclature is a subject for specialists, and quite a few mistakes appear even in fairly well-researched books on the subject.

We'll begin with the most basic, practical questions, and leave the subtler and more magical side of swordsmanship aside for a later point. What is a sword, and what are the parts that make it up? What types of sword can be used with the techniques in this book? What other equipment will you need for training? How is a sword held, and how is it drawn from the scabbard?

Naming The Sword

What is a sword? We can define the term, for our present purposes, as an edged weapon of metal in which the blade makes up by far the largest part of the total length. Even in the West, swords have been given a dizzying array of shapes and patterns, and the rest of the world can provide an even wider range of swords and swordlike weapons.

By the time the methods of swordsmanship covered in this book were developed, though, most of the more exotic Western sword types were things of the relatively distant past. What remained—leaving out the not-really-weapons used in sport fencing, and highly specialized dueling weapons such as the smallsword—was a handful of basic types, all of them fairly closely related. The most important distinction was between sabers, which had curved blades and a single sharp edge, and broadswords, which had straight blades and either one or two sharp edges. (Though the term "broadsword" is commonly used for medieval swords, this is inaccurate; it's an eighteenth-century word, and properly speaking applies to a particular class of eighteenth-, nineteenth- and early twentieth-century military swords.) Each of these two basic types had its variations, but essentially the same terminology and techniques could be used with any of them.

The parts of the sword are shown in diagram 2-1. The blade is the business end of the sword, and it's divided into the forte—the half closest to your hand, which is used for blocking and parrying an opponent's attacks—and the foible—the half furthest from your hand, which is used for dealing out cuts and thrusts of your own. The fuller is a groove running down the length of the blade; folklore has it that it's meant as a channel for blood, and the term "blood groove" gets used for it in some places, but it's actually a way of making a blade lighter without sacrificing strength. The edge, of course, is the part of the blade that's sharpened; if the blade has only one edge, the other side is called the back. If a small part of the back near the tip is sharpened, this area is called the false edge.

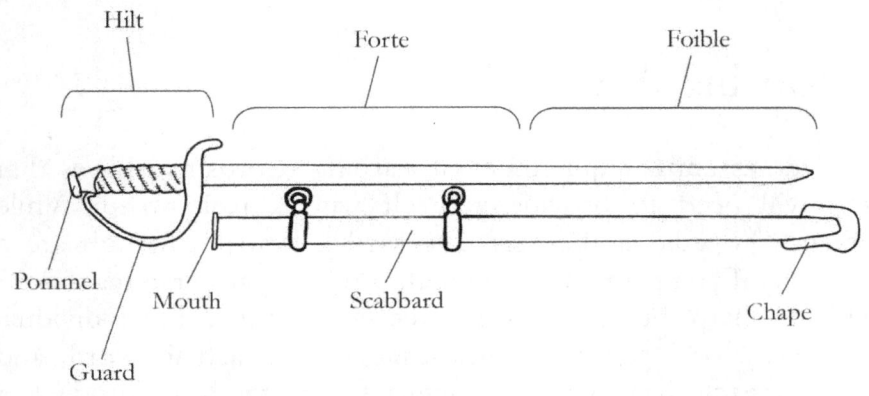

Diagram 2-1

The hilt is the entire apparatus on the end of the sword you grasp. Its parts include the guard, which is the arrangement of metal bars or plates protecting the hand, and can be anything from a plain crosspiece to an intricate pattern of defensive metalwork; the grip, which is the part held in the hand; and the pommel, at the end of the grip, which serves as a counterweight to balance the weight of the blade, and can also be used to deliver blows to an opponent's face and head in close combat. Running through the hilt is the tang, an extension of the blade; in a well-made sword, it goes all the way through to the pommel.

Some parts of the guard need to be named in more detail as well, although not all swords have them. Quillons are bars of metal, straight or curved, which extend out at right angles to the blade between blade and grip. A shell is a solid metal plate, usually curved, that protects all or part of the sword hand. A knuckle bow is a protective bar that curves around the hand from blade to pommel, guarding the fingers against a cut. The ultimate in hand protection is a basket hilt, of the sort most often seen on Scottish broadswords, which surrounds the entire hand with protective steel bars.

Finally, the scabbard is the case or sheath in which the blade is put when the sword's not in use. The opening of the scabbard is called the mouth, and the metal tip at the other end is called the chape.

Choosing A Sword

One essential requirement of learning swordsmanship is that you will need to provide yourself with a real sword. While practice swords of the sort discussed a little further on are a necessity if you plan on training safely with a partner, a real sword with a sharp blade of good steel is essential for individual practice. Nothing else handles quite like an actual sword, and training exclusively with a practice sword tends to produce a variety of bad habits in the student. Those who have studied the way subtle energies flow through different material substances—a branch of knowledge once known as natural magic—also know that tempered steel has subtle effects on energy and consciousness that no other substance can match. If you intend to master the sword in any real sense you will need a sword to master.

The exact type of sword you choose is open to a good deal of variation, and depends largely on your personal preferences and on the spiritual or magical tradition you practice. The tradition of swordsmanship taught in this book was intended to be used with the standard nineteenth-century infantry sword, which had a straight blade, a single sharpened edge, a sturdy back, and a hilt that offered some degree of hand protection. The same techniques, however, can be used with nearly any of the standard types of eighteenth- or nineteenth-century sword, from cavalry sabers through naval cutlasses to Highland Scots basket-hilted broadswords. With a few modifications, they can also be used with most other single-handed swords from any historical period.

Whatever type of sword you choose, though, you should

Chapter 2 – Fundamentals of Sword Training

purchase one that is a real weapon, not a toy. The spectacular growth of modern historical (and not so historical) reenactment groups has made for a much wider selection of swords than could be found as little as twenty years ago—any magazine devoted to this market will offer a remarkable selection of ads—but the quality of what's available varies just as widely. Some sources produce fine weapons, of a grade that warriors of past centuries would have been happy to own; others turn out useless lumps of pot metal, more dangerous to the wielder than to an opponent. You will need to tread carefully when shopping. A relatively plain sword of useable quality is likely to cost you from two to five hundred dollars at current prices; on the other hand, price alone is no guarantee that the weapon is worth buying and using.

Some of the points you should look for are the following:

1. The blade should be of good quality steel, not stainless steel, cast iron, or some pot metal alloy coated with chrome, and it should be forged and tempered, not just cast or machined into shape. Chrome plating is a reliable sign of poor quality; the blade should look like a good knife blade, not like a piece cut out of an old-fashioned car bumper! It must be flexible enough to bend slightly and still spring back straight—this is the classic test for a good temper—but strong enough not to droop under its own weight when held out horizontally. It should also be straight to start with, of course; if you hold the blade edge on and you can see wobbles or bends, you're looking at junk.

2. The blade should be capable of taking and holding a fine edge. This is one of the more difficult details to check on, since few makers of replica swords have ever put their blades to the test of cutting practice. Those that do commonly make much of the fact, and this can be a good sign that you're dealing with someone reputable. It's also useful to check the edge that the sword already has at the time of purchase; swordmakers who treat their products as real weapons, rather

than costume accessories, routinely put a respectable edge on their blades. While you're checking the edge, look along it for the telltale parallel scratches of machine grinding, a common mark of low-quality blades.

3. The guard and pommel may be of brass or steel. They should be sturdy and solidly made, but not overly heavy, and if ornamented, the decoration should be of a sort that won't catch clothing or interfere with the handling of the blade. All parts of the hilt should be firmly attached, so that they don't wobble.

4. The grip may be wood, ivory, or metal, and if it's wrapped, it may be wrapped with leather or metal wire—not with the cord or thread wrapping used on many cheap decorative swords, which will wear through quickly. In any case, the grip must be solidly connected to the tang, which should extend all the way through to the pommel. Grip the sword firmly in your sword hand, and shake. Any feeling of looseness, or any noticeable wobble in the join between blade and grip, is a problem. In some cases this can be fixed, by taking the hilt apart and inserting a thin piece of leather to take up the slack; in others, it's the product of shoddy workmanship, and there's not much you can do.

5. One critical point often neglected by the inexperienced has to do with the weight of the sword. Most actual fighting swords, in the days when swords were commonly used in combat, were very light—between one and a half and four pounds for a sword wielded with one hand—and the eighteenth- and nineteenth-century blades for which the techniques in this book were designed tend toward the lighter end of that range, due to improvements in the quality of steel at the time of the Industrial Revolution. Many modern replica swords, by contrast, are made to hang on walls, not to face the realities of combat. They are much heavier—from five to fifteen pounds, in many cases—which makes them effectively useless for

Chapter 2 – Fundamentals of Sword Training

anything but very specialized types of training. (Those are covered in Chapter Nine of this book.) When handling a sword, imagine yourself having to cut and thrust with it for an hour or two without stopping. Is it light enough to make that imaginable?

6. The sword should also have a scabbard, to keep it clean and safe, and it's a good idea to have a sword belt with the right fittings for hanging the sword at your side. It's worth mentioning that swords used according to the techniques in this book should traditionally be worn at your hip, not over the back the way those TV characters do. Over-the-back scabbards are strictly for two-handed swords, which are too long to wear at the side without dragging on the ground or sticking out a yard or so behind you. The traditional reason for insisting on a belt- carried sword is strictly practical: it's much quicker to draw a sword from your hip than over your shoulder, and in the lethal environment of sword combat the second or two you lose drawing a sword over your shoulder may be your last. The scabbard may be of leather or metal, and the sword belt should certainly be of sturdy leather, with solid metal fittings. A sword belt isn't strictly necessary for sword training, but you'll want it if you intend to learn the traditional method of drawing the sword, which is given a little later in this chapter.

7. Finally, it's usually a good idea to look for a replica sword that's a copy of an actual weapon in someone's collection, rather than one made to suit modern fashions. While the latter may look very impressive, they are usually designed by people who have no knowledge of actual combat swordsmanship, and they usually leave much to be desired when put to use in solo training or cutting practice.

If you're interested in an eighteenth- or nineteenth-century sword type, you have a certain advantage; historical reenactment groups devoted to the Revolutionary War, the Civil War, and other conflicts of the same epoch tend to be fanatical about accuracy—which means that swords marketed to these groups usually follow authentic and highly functional designs. If you're interested in medieval weaponry, on the other hand, expect to encounter a lot of flashy, useless, and historically preposterous junk, and a few competently made, historically accurate weapons. If the catalog or the swordmaker can give you a source for the design—especially if it's a source you could check up on if you wanted to—you're likely to be looking at something worth buying and using. If the design came out of a twenty-first-century head, on the other hand, it's anybody's guess.

Practice Swords

It cannot be said too strongly that an actual sword is only for solo practice. Too many modern people seem to think that a weapon that doesn't shoot bullets can't actually hurt anyone, and as a result an embarrassing number of people these days treat edged weapons as harmless fashion statements. Attitudes like these can be lethal in sword training. A solid cut with a sharp, well-made sword can literally cut a human body in half. Even a half-hearted cut or thrust, made as a joke, can leave your target bleeding to death or maimed for life. A fundamental rule in sword training is this: never swing or thrust a real sword at anyone unless you are prepared to face homicide charges.

Obviously, then, you'll need something other than a real sword when it comes time for you to practice with a partner. Some sort of practice sword should be on your shopping list as you get ready to train.

Several different types of practice swords can be used for partner training. In the lodge settings where this system of swordsmanship was once practiced, a specific kind of practice sword was standard equipment, although they apparently aren't made or sold nowadays. If you happen to know a friendly blacksmith or belong to a lodge that still has such equipment tucked away in a back closet, though, you might consider this style. The "combat sword," as it was called, had a heavy basket hilt of steel bars to protect the hand, and a light blade 18 to 20 inches long—only a little more than half the length of an ordinary sword—with a blunt point and dull edges.

This design allowed students to practice cuts, guards, thrusts and parries at the usual combat distance, with nothing but sword hands actually close enough to be hit—and those were fully protected by the basket hilt. In effect, on a combat sword the foible of the blade is only a few inches long; the rest is forte. It has certain drawbacks—sparring with combat swords doesn't entirely duplicate the experience of sparring with full-length blades, and can lead to bad habits if the differences aren't kept in mind. Still, the combat sword was an interesting and useful piece of equipment, and one that seems to have been completely forgotten by historians of swordsmanship.

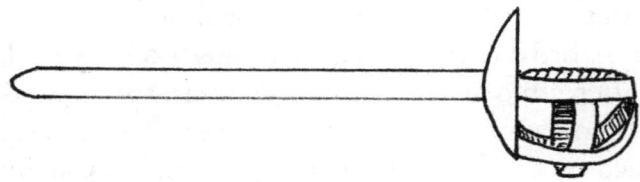

Diagram 2-2

Perhaps the best commonly available practice swords, if you can't obtain combat swords of the old style, are training swords made with blunted schlager blades. Heavier and less "whippy" than the blades used in modern sport fencing, schlager blades can be purchased for quite reasonable prices from makers of historical replica weapons. For safety, the tip should be covered with a rubber blunt, which can be bought at any archery supply store. If you can manage this, your schlager blade should be fitted on a hilt of the same type as your sword's, and the length of the blade should be approximately the same; this will provide you with very nearly the best possible equivalent of live steel.

Not as good as schlager blades, but still quite useable for training purposes, are fencing sabres. These have relatively stiff, straight blades that make a fairly good imitation of a real sword, and they will stand up well to the strain of combat, although they tend to be overly light. The tip should always be covered with a proper sabre tip for safety.

Another option, although it's not as good a choice as the ones already mentioned, are shinai, the bamboo training swords used in Japanese swordsmanship. These are quite safe and fairly sturdy. They are much too light, however, and don't handle like a real sword. Getting one of the proper length for a Western sword is also a problem, since katana lengths (matching the Japanese longsword) are usually too long, and wakizashi (sized to the Japanese shortsword) are much too short.

Less useful for following the instructions in this book are swords made of wood or rattan, of the sort used by some medieval reenactment groups. These do a fair job of duplicating the characteristics of the heavier medieval weapons, but they aren't safe to use without full body armor. Fighting in armor is a different matter entirely from fighting without it, and since the system of swordsmanship taught in this book was developed centuries after armor went out of use, there seems little value in making students use it when there are other alternatives.

Not recommended at all, unless you can't get anything else, are "boffers"—swords made of foam padding over vinyl tubing, usually covered with a layer of duct tape to hold them together and resist wear. These have become very popular in some medieval reenactment circles, and they do have some advantages, as they're easy and inexpensive to make, and extremely safe to use. On the other hand, the combination of low weight and high air resistance means that they don't move like a real sword, and they can also be wielded with a fraction of the strength required by a real sword. If you train exclusively with boffers, you're unlikely to develop the physical strength and quick reflexes that are essential to actual swordsmanship, and you're likely to develop bad habits that can get you in real trouble when sparring with anything more realistic.

On the other hand, several groups dedicated to the revival of Western swordsmanship have devised foam-padded weapons with heavier, more rigid cores and shaped blades. These are said to handle much more like real swords. I haven't had the opportunity to work with these myself, and for that reason can't offer a blanket endorsement of them, but they represent an option well worth exploring.

Protective Gear

With the exception of boffers and shinai, the practice swords just described can still do a fair amount of damage to an unprotected human body. Some sort of protective gear is therefore a must.

The first requirement is protection for the eyes and face, which are the most vulnerable parts of your body to a stray sword thrust. There is only one worthwhile option here, and that is a good "three-weapon" (i.e., safe for foil, epee, and sabre) fencing mask. Get one that fits your head properly, and wear it whenever you cross swords with another person, even as a joke. Neglect of this very simple but very necessary rule has caused blindings and deaths; it takes very little force for a sword, even a practice sword, to penetrate an eyeball, and not much more for it to break through the eye socket into the brain.

Along with the mask, a sturdy leather glove to protect your sword hand, a cup to protect your groin, and (if you are female) breast protectors to shield the sensitive tissue there, are well worth having. There's much to be said for the sport fencing kit as a standard uniform for sword practice; the heavy canvas jacket will spare you the worst of the bruising that even blunt-edged swords can deal out, and it's designed not to provide any place for a stray sword point to catch and penetrate. A complete set of fencing gear of reasonable quality—glove, jacket, and three-weapon mask—can be had for less than two hundred dollars as of this writing, and the investment may well be worth making if you intend to study the sword with any degree of seriousness.

Even with protective gear of this sort, you can expect to suffer bruises and other minor injuries now and then. If you intend to practice swordsmanship, that's part of the bargain.

Remember that the skills you are learning were created by people seeking the most efficient way to damage other human beings with a long piece of metal.

Holding The Sword

Different traditions of swordsmanship have different ways of grasping the sword hilt, and each has its advantages and disadvantages. Be this as it may, the system presented in this book uses a very specific way of holding the sword. It's important to learn and practice it, rather than simply grabbing the sword all anyhow; many of the techniques and tactics discussed later on in this book depend on the proper connection between the hand and the sword, and can't be done as effectively if the hilt is grasped in a different way.

The proper way to hold your sword is shown in Diagram 2-3. The grip should be practiced regularly, so that you can grip a sword this way without having to think about where your fingers go. The key points are these:

1. The thumb is on the back of the hilt, resting against the guard and pressing the grip down against the fingers. Many eighteenth- and nineteenth-century swords were made with a hollow or flat place at the point where the thumb comes to rest, to maximize the advantages of this position.

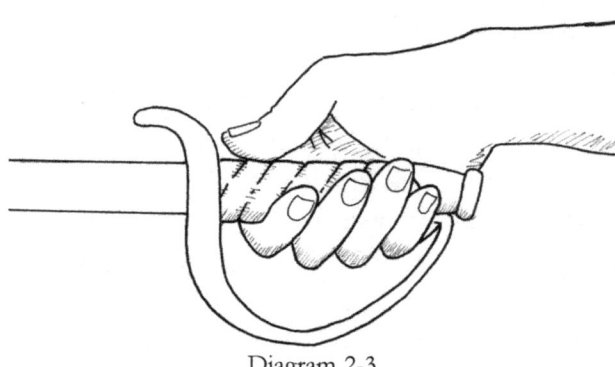

Diagram 2-3

2. The fingers are curled comfortably around the grip. Try to avoid a "death grip" on the hilt; your hand should hold the sword firmly but flexibly.

3. The hand as a whole is positioned close to the pommel, rather than being brought up close to the guard.

When held this way, the hilt of the sword becomes a lever balanced between your thumb and your index finger, and it takes very little effort to push the lever back and forth or twist it around as needed. This gives you a great deal of control over the blade, and allows for the precision that swordsmanship requires. This way of holding the sword should thus be used at all times except when you have the sword at the carry, as described in Chapter Six, or in a few other situations we'll discuss as we come to them.

Most people, of course, will hold the sword in the right hand. You may find it best to take a few moments, though, to try it in either hand. Handedness in swords doesn't always follow handedness in other things; the present author, for example, is left-handed in most things but right-handed with a sword. If you do turn out to handle a sword best left-handed, you'll need to reverse all the directions for position and movement in the chapters to come.

You should also consider training with both hands, whether or not you ever intend to use a sword with your weak hand. The effort necessary for most people to teach their weak hand to use a sword pays off in increased coordination and precision with the strong hand; most people can fake their way through a technique with their strong hand, but to do it with either hand requires that the technique actually be understood.

There's also a broader issue here. Developing the body in a one-sided way is bad for health as well as esthetics. It's recorded that King Richard III of England spent so much time in his youth practicing swordsmanship with his right hand that he ended up with one shoulder higher than the other, and the nickname of "Crookback." There's no good reason to do the same to yourself.

Drawing The Sword

Different swords are equipped with different devices that allow them to hang at your hip. Depending on what sort of sword you've chosen, you may be dealing with anything from a double- wrapped medieval sword belt to the clever and efficient arrangement of hooks and straps used in nineteenth-century military gear. Nearly any system for supporting a sword, though, can be used with the method of drawing the sword covered here.

One detail that sometimes confuses beginners, and should be mentioned at this point, has to do with which side the sword is worn on. If you are right-handed with a sword, you should wear the sword on your left hip; if you're left-handed, conversely, wear the sword on your right. Reaching across the body to draw the sword puts the blade at an angle that allows it to be drawn quickly and easily, and it also means that the blade is slanting across your body, providing some degree of protection for your vital organs, even before the tip leaves the scabbard.

To draw the sword, then, take hold of the scabbard just below the mouth with your off hand—your left hand, assuming that you're right-handed with a sword. Tilt the mouth of the scabbard forward. Reach across your body with your sword hand and grasp the hilt, palm down, so that your thumb is on the end closest to the scabbard and your little finger on the end furthest away. When you first grasp the sword, your thumb does not go on the back of the hilt; let it rest on the side of the grip closest to your body, where it won't interfere with the process of drawing.

Now pull the sword up and out until the tip clears the mouth of the scabbard, as shown. The arm should be extended freely, and the sword drawn in a straight line, as though you were trying to hit someone in the face with the pommel. (In fact, this was a technique that was sometimes used when drawing a sword against an opponent who was trying to rush in.)

Now snap the sword up, over and down in an arc by turning your wrist, and in the process, put your thumb on the back of the hilt where it belongs. This motion can easily be extended into a cut, and followed up by a moulinet (described in Chapter Six). This makes an effective way to respond to an opponent who attacks as you draw your sword. If you don't face a situation of this sort, simply bring your sword hand back and down and take up the engaging guard or the hanging guard, as described in Chapter Seven.

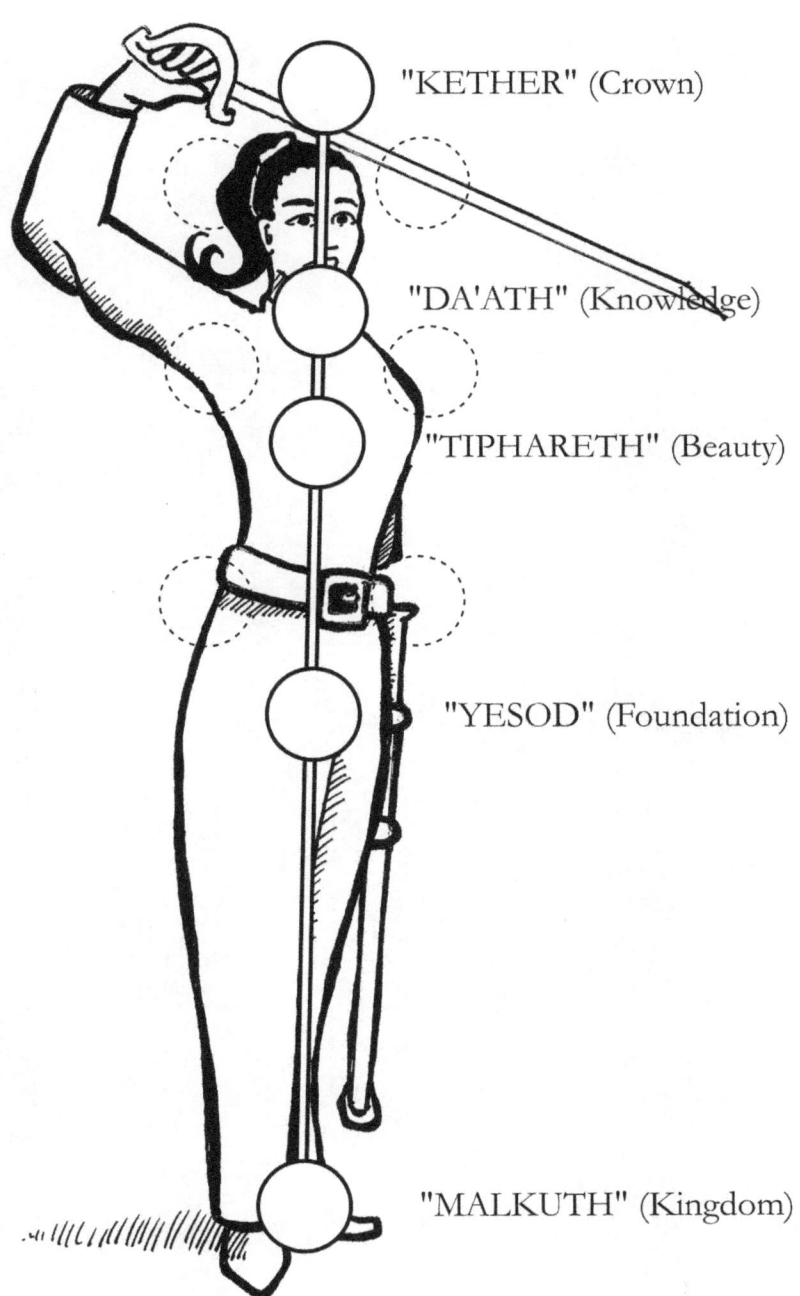

The Middle Pillar of the Tree of Life
Within the Body of a Swordswoman

Chapter Three
fundamental exercises

It's a central principle in all martial arts, in East and West alike, that the weapon in the hand must become an extension of the body. In the inner martial arts, in turn, this principle is taken further, and the body itself is understood as an extension of the spirit, focused through a variety of levels of consciousness and being.

Training the higher levels of mind and personality to reflect the spirit is the goal of the world's spiritual paths, and the basic disciplines of every mystical tradition are aimed toward this goal. There is a vast arsenal of practices and disciplines that will not be covered here, partly because different students follow different traditions, partly because this book is a manual of one forgotten Western martial art, not an encyclopedia of every conceivable spiritual path!

If you wish to pursue this broader work, the necessary philosophy and techniques can be learned from qualified teachers or, in some traditions, studied and learned from books on the subject. In many of the Western inner traditions, in particular, the essential practices—concentration, meditation, and energy practices such as the Middle Pillar exercise—have long been taught by way of written lessons rather than personal instruction, and can readily be learned from a range of books in print, including several by the present author.

The body, however, is where the connection between the warrior and the weapon takes place. In many ways, it is the crucial link in the movement of intention from the spirit to the sword. It requires specialized training in order to meet the challenges of any martial art. The core methods of that training are an essential part of an education in swordsmanship, and are covered in detail in the next three chapters.

Exercise For Swordsmanship

Certain misunderstandings have to be avoided at the outset. It's important to distinguish the physical training needed for swordsmanship and other martial arts, for example, from the sort of "conditioning" that goes on at most gyms nowadays. For more than half a century now, the standard bodybuilding exercises have focused on the appearance of strength and health instead of the reality.

Even when steroids and other health-damaging chemicals aren't used, as they so often are, people who follow this sort of training use methods that produce muscle mass without actually developing strength or stamina. In sports medicine jargon, modern bodybuilding methods produce sarcoplasmotic hypertrophy, which means that the muscle tissue is simply inflated with fluid, which does nothing for strength or efficiency. The goal of serious, traditional exercises systems is sarcofibril hypertrophy, which means that the muscle tissue adds more contractile fibers and thus increases in real strength. Exercises that produce the one don't produce the other, and vice versa.

The result of today's bodybuilding methods, in most cases, is a body covered with masses of swollen, puffy muscle tissue, impressive to look at but useless for anything but posing on a stage. It should be obvious that there's no place for this sort of cosmetic approach in a martial arts training regimen, and if you intend to take up swordsmanship, you're probably better off staying far away from your local gym. The sort of classical weight training regimen used by old-time strongmen and the physical culture movement of the late nineteenth and early twentieth century is another matter entirely, but you won't find methods of this sort being taught at your local health club.

The type of physical training needed for any given martial art depends on the particular needs and approaches of the art in question. Some arts demand a great deal of physical strength and stamina, others require flexibility and quickness, while still others need sensitivity to subtle energy and the capacity to move with force rather than against it, which is acquired by relaxation and gentleness.

Since a sword amplifies the force put into it manyfold by means of leverage, and can deal out devastating blows even when handled with very modest strength, the tradition of swordsmanship we're exploring here doesn't call for any great amount of physical force. Flexibility, quickness, sensitivity and relaxation are all necessary in somewhat larger degrees. More than these, however, the art we'll be studying require poise, precision, and economy of motion.

Some people are born with these capacities, but most aren't. Inborn talent isn't necessary, however. Just as wrestling builds strength, and t'ai chi builds softness and sensitivity, the practice of sword training—carried out steadily, patiently and systematically—will build the capacities that lead to mastery. A foundation for practice, though, can speed the process of training and developing the body into an effective tool for the mind and spirit, and for this reason certain basic physical exercises have an important place.

Ten Fundamental Exercises

The first and most fundamental of these elementary steps on the Path is a set of ten fundamental exercises, which stretch, tone and strengthen the muscles of the trunk and spine. Beyond their value as preparation for swordsmanship, these exercises are an excellent way to improve overall health and fitness, as well as a good foundation for certain kinds of inner training. They are particularly useful as a preparation for the Middle Pillar exercise, a fundamental practice in some of the main Western inner traditions.

These exercises focus almost entirely on the central axis of the body. Imagine a line extending from the top of the skull straight down through the neck, the ribcage, and the abdomen to the open space in the center of the pelvis, just in front of the tailbone; from there, in a standing body, it continues straight down between the legs to a point between the feet. From this line, and especially from the portion of it that runs from the underside of the skull to the base of the pelvis, all physical movement unfolds.

The same line also traces out the Middle Pillar, (see diagram on page 39) the most important channel through which the body's subtle energies flow, and the body's five principal energy centers—at the crown of the head, the middle of the throat, the heart, the genitals, and the feet—all center on the Middle Pillar. By working with the body structures surrounding this central axis, stretching and toning the muscles and ligaments of the torso, and breaking down unnecessary tensions all through the region, these exercises thus clear away the most important barriers to the free movement of the body and its subtle energies alike.

Once learned, the complete set of exercises takes around ten minutes to perform. The full set should be done regularly once a day, preferably first thing in the morning, and can also be used as a good set of warmup exercises before each session of sword practice. Simple as they may seem, these exercises should not be passed over or neglected, for much of the material in this book depends on the results you'll get by regularly practicing them. If you learn them now, and spend a week or two practicing them before going further, you'll be making an investment of time that will pay off substantially in terms of later achievement.

I've given a recommended number of repetitions for each exercise, but this is subject to plenty of exceptions. Above all, you should pay attention to your own physical condition, and set your sights accordingly. The exercises are not particularly strenuous, but if you are not in good physical condition when you start, you may find it better to decrease the repetitions at first. You may also need to start off practicing them once every other day, or at longer intervals, if your body is in poor shape.

It's important not to let your ego get in the way of a realistic judgment of your condition, or to think that it's no use even trying if you can't manage some arbitrary level of performance to start with. Even if you can only do one repetition of each exercise, once a week, that's fine—that will build strength and stamina, and help you achieve more later on. There's no benefit to be gained by pushing yourself to the point of injury. The old alchemical motto is worth remembering: festina lente—make haste slowly!

First fundamental exercise:

On the physical level, this exercise develops healthy posture, and tones the muscles of the arms and shoulders; on a subtler level, it works with the heart or Tiphareth center of the Middle Pillar.

Stand straight with your heels touching and your toes turned out at a 45-degree angle to each side. Your spine should be straight but not stiff, with your head held as though you had a cup full of water balanced on top and you were trying not to spill a drop. Raise your arms out to the sides until they reach straight out from your shoulders, elbows and wrists straight but not stiffened, palms forward, fingers and thumbs together. This is the basic position for all the exercises.

Diagram 3-1

Now, without changing the position of your body, legs or head, bring your hands quickly down to rest on your hips, fingers forward and thumbs pointing back, elbows out to the sides, as shown in Diagram 3-2. At once, bring your arms quickly back to the basic position shown in Diagram 3-1.

Diagram 3-2

Then bring your hands up and in to touch the back of your head, as shown in Diagram 3-3. Again, your body, legs and head should not change position, and your elbows should stay extended out to the sides. At once, return to the basic position.

Diagram 3-3

Then let your arms arc down smoothly to your sides, and raise them back up again to the basic position. This completes one cycle of the first exercise; ten cycles completes the set.

Unlike the other exercises, which are done smoothly and slowly, this one should be done quickly, letting the arms snap from position to position. Breathing should be smooth and even throughout.

Second fundamental exercise:

On the physical level, this exercise works the shoulders, arms, and upper back; on a subtler level, it works with the throat or Daath center of the Middle Pillar. Starting again in the basic position, turn your hands palm up, and then move them backwards as far as you comfortably can. Then circle your arms and hands up, forward, down and back, tracing out a circle about a foot in diameter with your fingertips. Your elbows and wrists should remain straight; all movement comes from the shoulders. Circle one way ten times, then reverse the movement ten times. Breathing and movement alike should be slow, smooth and even.

Diagram 3-4

Third fundamental exercise:

This exercise is intended to complement the second exercise; on the physical level, it works a different set of muscles in the shoulders and upper back, tones the calves, and helps develop balance. In the realm of subtle energy, it primarily works with the Daath or throat center of the Middle Pillar, but it also has positive effects on the Kether center at the crown of the head and the Malkuth center at the level of the soles of the feet.

Starting from the basic position again, turn your hands palm down. Then raise your arms up to a 45-degree angle, and at the same time rise up on your toes, as in Diagram 3-5. Lower your arms to the level of the basic position, and at the same time come down from your toes to rest both feet flat on the ground. Repeat a total of ten times. Breathing is synchronized with the movement: breathe in when you rise up, breathe out when you come back down. The movements themselves should be slow and even. Be careful not to raise your arms higher than a 45-degree angle, or to lower them past horizontal; either of these mistakes will lose some of the potential benefit of the exercise.

Diagram 3-5

Fourth fundamental exercise:

On the physical level, this exercise develops the all-important muscles of the waist, abdomen and lower back, and also helps to strengthen and tone the neck. On a subtler level, it works with the Daath center at the throat and the Yesod center at the genitals. Begin in the basic position, and then place your hands on the back of your head, as in the second part of the first exercise. Then bend forward at the hips, keeping your legs and lower back straight, and at the same time arch your neck so that your face keeps facing forward rather than down, as shown in diagram 3-6.

Diagram 3-6

Then straighten up again, straightening your neck in the same movement, and lean back from the hips, arching your back and keeping your legs straight. While doing so, tuck your chin and bend your neck forward, so that once again your face keeps facing forward, as shown in diagram 3-7.

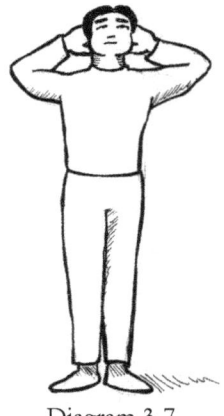

Diagram 3-7

One bend forward and one bend backward completes one cycle. Do ten cycles. The movement is smooth and easy throughout. Breathing is synchronized with the movement: breathe out as your body moves forward, in as it moves backward. Be sure not to close your throat or hold your breath at any point.

Fifth fundamental exercise:

On the physical level, this exercise works the muscles of the sides of the torso, stretches the spine, and also strengthens the neck. On a subtler level, it works with the Daath center at the neck and the Yesod center at the genitals.

Start from the basic position. Raise your right arm up until it it extended straight up from the shoulder, and then bend it over the top of your head, until your right fingers rest flat against your left ear; at the same time, lower your left arm to your side. Then bend slowly to the left from the waist, and let your left hand slide down the outside of your leg. Your legs and hips should remain motionless, and your body and head should lean only to the side, not forward or back.

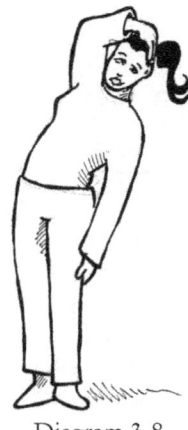

Diagram 3-8

Then straighten up slowly, and bring your arms back to the basic position. Next do the same movement on the other side, raising the left arm up and over the head, lowering the right arm to the side, and bending slowly and smoothly to the right. Then straighten up and return to the basic position. One bend each way completes one cycle. Do five cycles, breathing in as you raise your arm up and over, and out as you bend to the side.

Sixth fundamental exercise:

On a physical level, this exercise expands the chest, develops the middle back and the muscles of the spine, and tones the diaphragm. On a subtler level, it works with the Daath and Tiphareth centers at throat and heart respectively, and also has important effects on the subsidiary energy centers in the palms of the hands.

Begin in the basic position. Form your hands into fists and draw them in to your sides, turning the knuckles down and pointing the elbows back. Then arch the back and neck, drawing the shoulders and elbows back and inward and the head back, breathing in deeply and steadily, and stretching the chest, as shown in diagram 3-9.

Diagram 3-9

Next, straighten the back and neck and push the hands straight forward until the arms are extended horizontally in front of you, opening the hands and turning them until the palms face down, with the fingers stretched forward. As you do this, tuck your chin slightly, stretching the back of the neck. The resulting position is shown in diagram 3-10. Then sweep your arms out to the sides, returning to the basic position.

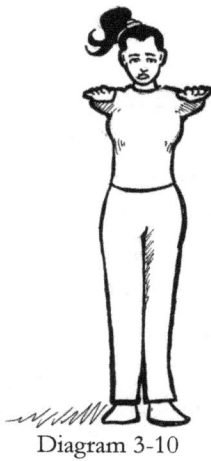
Diagram 3-10

Do ten cycles of this exercise. Breathe in deeply as you draw your fists in and arch your back, and breathe out when you extend the arms forward and then out to the sides. Fill your lungs to the utmost on the inbreath, but be careful not to close your throat or hold your breath at any point.

Seventh fundamental exercise:

On the physical level, this exercise works the legs, hips and lower back, and also builds balance and poise; on a subtler level, it works with the Yesod center at the genitals and the Malkuth center between the feet. Start in the basic position, and then move one foot about fifteen inches to the side, standing as in diagram 3-11. Then bend your knees and lower your body slowly and evenly, coming up onto your toes as you do so, until your knees are fully bent, as in diagram 3-12. Your body should not lean forward or back, and your arms should stay extended out to the sides. Rise up again, slowly and smoothly, until your knees are straight and your feet are flat on the floor. Repeat ten times, breathing out as you descend and in as you rise.

Diagram 3-11   Diagram 3-12

This can be a difficult exercise to do if you don't have good balance and stamina, or if your legs or knees are weak. An easier version can help you build up the strength and poise you need to do it as given. For this, you'll need a chair or another piece of furniture, tall enough that you can take hold of the top without bending forward, and stable enough that you can trust your weight to it without tipping it over. (A bedroom dresser works well for many people.) Stand in front of it in the starting position and take a solid grip on the top. Then bend your knees and rise up on your toes, lowering yourself with your back straight, as shown in diagram 3-13.

Diagram 3-13

Go as far as you can without causing pain or feeling that your legs are about to give way. Rise up again, straightening your legs and lowering your heels, until you are standing straight again, and then repeat. When you can do this ten times confortably, try lowering yourself further the next time. Once you are getting all the way down, shift more and more of your weight off your arms and onto your legs, and concentrate on doing the exercise smoothly and with balance. Once you can do this, you're ready to do without the furniture.

Eighth fundamental exercise:

On the physical level, this exercise works the muscles of the waist, the sides of the torso, and the lower back. On a subtler level, it concentrates on the main channel of the Middle Pillar, which connects all five of the centers, and also has important effects on the two centers at the ends of the Pillar, the Kether center at the crown of the head and the Malkuth center between the feet.

Start in the basic position, and then raise your arms up, clasping your hands above your head. Keep your elbows straight, so that your arms are pressed against your ears. Next, bending only at the waist, move your hands in a clockwise circle above your head, as shown in diagram 3-14. You'll know you're doing it right when the movement feels as though you're wringing the muscles of the sides and abdomen.

Be sure that you bend an equal amount back, forward, and to each side. Your legs and hips should not move at all, your elbows remain straight and your shoulders do not shift; the muscles of the waist, sides and lower back do all the work. Do five circles clockwise, and then five counterclockwise.

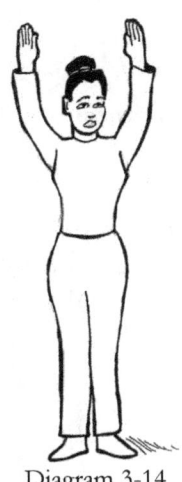

Diagram 3-14

Ninth fundamental exercise:

On the physical level, this very thorough exercise stretches and tones the muscles all along the spine, as well as the shoulders, hips, and legs; on a subtle level, it works with the entire Middle Pillar, involving all five centers and the connecting channel between them. Start in the basic position, and then, as in the seventh exercise, move one foot fifteen or so inches to the side.

Without moving your feet or turning your head, turn your shoulders and trunk to the left, so that your right arm extends straight in front of you and your left arm straight back, as in diagram 3-15; your eyes still look straight ahead, and your right shoulder comes close to your chin.

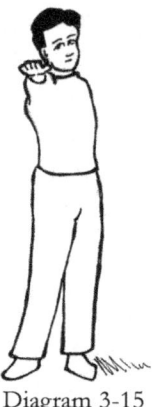

Diagram 3-15

From this position, bend forward at the waist, flexing your right knee slightly if necessary, so that your right hand traces an arc straight down and touches the ground between your feet, while your left arm extends straight above you, as in diagram 3-16.

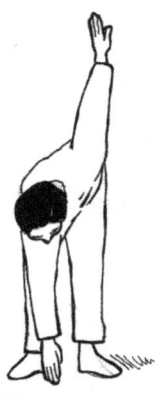

Diagram 3-16

Then move your right arm and hand out and up to the right, straightening up as you do so. Follow the movement of your hand with your eyes, so that you end up in a posture that differs from the basic position only in that you're looking toward your right hand, as shown in diagram 3-17. Finally, turn your head to look forward.

Diagram 3-17

Then repeat the entire process on the other side: turn your shoulders to the right so that your left hand comes forward; bend forward and flex your left knee slightly, so that your left hand touches the floor between your feet; take your left arm and hand out in an arc to the left, following it with your eyes and straightening up, and then looking forward. Once to each side makes once cycle of this exercise; do ten cycles, moving smoothly and steadily, breathing out as you turn your shoulders to the side and bend forward, and breathing in as you straighten back up again.

Tenth fundamental exercise:

This final exercise, on the physical level, works the abdomen and lower back, the shoulders and arms, and the neck, and it also makes the entire spine straight and flexible. On the subtler level, it circulates etheric energy out through the entire body.

Start in the basic position, and then raise your arms up in an arc to either side until they are extended straight above your head. Then bend forward at the waist, arching your neck as you did in the fourth exercise, so that you continue to face forward. At the same time, sweep your arms down, back and up until they are extended above and behind your back, as in diagram 3-18.

Diagram 3-18

Then bring your arms down, forward and up, straightening your waist and neck, so that you are standing upright again with your arms reaching up above your head as before. Finally, return to the basic position. Do the whole process five times.

The breathing in this exercise is the most important part, since it's by deep steady breathing that the body's subtle energies are put in motion and circulated through the body as a whole. Your breaths here should be slow, steady and full. Breathe in as you raise your arms, out as you bend forward, in again as you straighten up, and out again as you lower your arms to the basic position.

Chapter Four
relaxation and breathing exercises

The development of muscles, ligaments, and tendons carried out by way of the preparatory exercises in Chapter Three establishes the physical foundation for working with a sword. In the teachings of the Western world's inner traditions, though, the physical level is seen as only the densest and most inert of a whole spectrum of levels of existence. The body, similarly, is not simply a lump of meat and bone, but a complex pattern of forms and forces operating on many levels of reality. Moving through it, and playing a crucial part in its effective functioning, are currents of subtle energy.

There are various names for the subtle energy of life in the inner traditions of the West. The one we'll be using in this book, one of the most common in modern times, is etheric energy. (Those who have studied Asian martial arts will be more familiar with terms such as ch'i or ki, which refer to exactly the same thing.) Even on a physical level, the human body is as much a pattern of etheric forces as a material object—a point that Asian systems of healing such as acupuncture (as well as their forgotten Western equivalents) show with great clarity. Training the subtle flows of etheric energy through the body is thus as critical a foundation for effective swordsmanship as training the muscles.

Relaxation

The first step toward working with the subtle etheric flows in the body is learning to relax. Most people, most of the time, carry a great deal of unnecessary muscular tension in their bodies. This gets in the way of the free flow of etheric energy, producing blockages and distortions that are a major cause of disease. Even in a purely physical sense, excess tension is a bad idea for a student of swordsmanship, as it makes movements slow, stiff and heavy, preventing the body from achieving the precision and speed that sword combat requires.

It actually takes a certain amount of work to learn to relax. Start by getting into loose, comfortable clothing, and lying down on your back on a hard surface. This usually means the bare floor. Your bed is out, and so is anything else comfortably padded; if you have a hardwood floor available, that is best, but a carpeted floor will do if the carpet's not too thick. (If the only floor available is bare concrete, this will also do, but you should spread a thin blanket on it to keep it from absorbing heat too quickly from your body and chilling your muscles.)

Odds are, if you haven't practiced relaxation before, that you'll find lying on a hard surface fairly uncomfortable. The places that hurt are the places where you have plenty of excess tension built up. Do your best to put up with the discomfort; you'll find that the more you practice relaxation, the less uncomfortable that hard surface will feel.

First relaxation exercise:

The first step in learning to relax is to pay attention to where you aren't relaxed. Start by noticing how much of your body is actually touching the floor. Most people who haven't learned to relax hold themselves up off the floor on a few points—the back of the head, the shoulderblades, the middle of the back, the buttocks, the calves, the heels. If that's the way you are lying, imagine just how much effort it's taking you to support the weight of your body on those few points. That's a good measure of the amount of muscular energy you're wasting in useless tension.

Spend a few moments trying to sink down onto the floor, to broaden those few areas of contact, so that more of you is resting on the floor. Don't try to do this by adding more muscular effort! Simply let your body spread out and sink; breathe slowly and evenly, and imagine tension leaving your body on each outbreath. Don't worry if you don't manage much improvement at first. Like so much in swordsmanship, this has to be learned gradually, one step at a time.

Now turn your attention to your feet, and relax them in the same way, imagining yourself breathing out tension on every outbreath. Go from the feet to the ankles, and do the same thing. From the ankles proceed to the lower legs, the knees, the thighs, the buttocks, the groin, the hips, the abdomen (front and back together), the midriff (ditto), the ribcage (ditto). Then start again at the hands: relax the hands, the wrists, the lower arms, the elbows, the upper arms, the shoulder joints, and the upper part of the torso where the shoulders join the chest. Then go on to the neck, the jaw, the face, the scalp, finishing at the very top of the head.

The first few times you work your way through this process, you may notice only a small lessening of tension—or you may feel as limp as a boiled noodle! Either way, stretch, shift, and wiggle to wake up your muscles before you get up. You'll find that most of your tensions will slip right back into place before long...but not quite all of them. By practicing this relaxation exercise once a day, you'll find that your body is gradually learning how to do without all that tension, and the results will show in your sword training and the rest of your life.

Second relaxation exercise:

Once you have achieved some success with the first relaxation exercise, and can relax the different parts of your body more or less at will, you're ready to replace it with the second exercise. Begin as before, lying on your back on a hard surface, and allow your body to spread and sink, releasing the tension that holds it up off the floor. Then, as before, turn your attention to your feet. This time, though, start by tensing your feet. Without moving them, tense the muscles in them as forcefully as you can, so that they are completely stiff. Hold the tension for a few moments, and then relax them thoroughly, allowing the extra tension as well as their ordinary load of tension to drain away.

When the feet are as completely relaxed as you can manage, go on to the ankles; tense them, hold the tension for a few moments, and then relax them completely. Proceed up the body, just as in the first relaxation exercises, first tensing and then relaxing every part of your body, and finishing with the top of your head. As with the first exercise, practice this once a day.

This more advanced relaxation exercise helps develop the skills by which relaxation can be put to work, in swordsmanship and in daily life. It's not very useful to be able to relax completely, if that's all you can do; going totally limp is not that effective a strategy for general use. You also need to be able to tense different muscles at will, to the exact degree of tension needed, and to release the tension at once when it's no longer necessary. The alternate tensing and relaxing of this exercise helps develop this skill.

Breathing

Relaxation is an important element in etheric work, but the most important way that we interact with etheric energy is through our breathing. Deep, smooth, steady and even breathing tends to gather etheric energy and circulate it freely through the body. Shallow, ragged and hurried breathing disperses etheric energy and deprives the body of the life-force it needs. Learning to breathe well, then, is a crucial step toward learning to use the body well.

Most people in the West are very poor at breathing—after all, it's not something that we teach our children, or pay much attention to ourselves! As with the physical requirements of swordsmanship, though, exercises can help develop the necessary breathing skills.

The first two breathing exercises that follow should be done once each day. It's a good idea to do them right before, or right after, the relaxation exercises just given. They should not be done within an hour of eating, as breathing exercises on a full stomach can cause indigestion and nausea.

First breathing exercise:

Sit on a chair of comfortable height, with your feet and knees together, your hands on your thighs, your spine straight but not stiff, and your chin very slightly tucked in toward your neck. Your back should not be resting against the back of the chair at all; if you tend to slump backwards, sit on the front edge of the chair, and pay attention to keeping your spine upright. Your clothes should be comfortable and loose, especially around the waist and chest; tight belts and (if you are female) tight bras are particularly to be avoided.

Diagram 4-1

This is the basic posture for meditation in Western esoteric lore, and it has a number of advantages and useful effects. For our present purposes, though, its chief value is that it frees the breathing apparatus and allows a healthy circulation of etheric energy through the body.

To begin the exercise, empty your lungs as completely as possible, and keep them empty for a short time. Then breathe in, slowly and smoothly, through your nose; your mouth should remain shut throughout all these breathing exercises. Draw the breath down as far as possible at first, pressing down and out with your diaphragm, so that your belly expands while your chest remains motionless. Then, as your diaphragm reaches its full expansion, expand the middle section of your trunk, around the solar plexus and the floating ribs; finally, once this is full, expand your chest, feeling the outward stretch of the ribs and the breastbone.

These three phases should all be parts of a single motion of the breath, which starts in the lower abdomen and rises up to the upper chest. You'll know that you're doing it correctly when your belly draws slightly inwards as the upper part of your chest fills with air.

At this point, hold the breath you've taken for a short time. This should be done by maintaining the expansion of the muscles of the trunk, not by closing the throat. (If you close your throat while holding your breath in exercises such as these, you risk damaging the delicate internal structures of your lungs.) To check whether your throat is open, contract the muscles of your belly suddenly and sharply; the motion should force air out through your throat and nostrils.

Then breathe out by drawing your belly and diaphragm inwards and upwards, leaving your chest expanded. This should be done slowly and smoothly, without gasping. Finally, when the lungs are completely empty, keep them that way for a short time—again, this should be done with the muscles of the chest and abdomen, not by closing the throat—and then begin again with the inbreath.

This way of breathing is called the Complete Breath, because it brings fresh air into every part of your lungs, maximizing the amount of oxygen in your blood and the amount of etheric energy in your body's subtle channels. The Complete Breath is the healthiest way of breathing, and it opens the door to a variety of attainments, some physical, some more subtle. If you practice it regularly, you'll find that after a time your ordinary breathing begins to follow the same pattern. This is an excellent sign, and leads to improved health.

At first, if you have no previous experience with breathing exercises, two or three cycles of this exercise are enough. You should be careful not to do it so slowly that you end up gasping for air at the end, as this undoes much of the good done by the exercise. Pace yourself, breathing as slowly as you can without running out of air, and gradually increasing the number of cycles and the amount of time taken in each breath. Twenty cycles at a session is enough for most purposes.

Second breathing exercise:

When you can comfortably do ten cycles of the first breathing exercise at a pace of no more than six cycles a minute, you're ready to learn to the second, which is more demanding. The posture is the same as for the first.

For this exercise, start with a few cycles of the Complete Breath, then empty the lungs. Draw a breath into the upper chest, expanding the ribs and breastbone, but leaving the diaphragm drawn up and the belly in. Then, holding the breath by means of the expansion of the muscles, push the breath slowly down the trunk into the abdomen, lowering the diaphragm, pushing out the belly and allowing the chest to contract. Then shift the breath slowly back up into the chest, without letting any of it go. Repeat, shifting the breath down into the belly and then back up into the chest, a total of five times. Then breathe out slowly and smoothly, just as in the Complete Breath. Repeat.

With this exercise, it's absolutely critical that you hold the breath with the muscles of the chest and abdomen rather than by closing the throat. It's also important to pace yourself, to avoid gasping or running out of air, and to move the breath up and down gently rather than with excessive force. Slow and easy does it! Start out with only one or two cycles, and gradually build up to five, which is enough for our purposes. (More than five cycles a day can overload your system, and should not be done except under the guidance of an experienced practitioner.)

If you feel pain or serious discomfort in your stomach a few hours after performing this exercise, this is a sign that you have put too much muscular force into the exercise. In this case, you should stop all breathing exercises for at least two weeks to allow your body to recover, and start again gradually and gently. If the discomfort persists for more than a short time, or becomes increasingly severe, you should see a qualified medical practitioner immediately.

Once you can do the second breathing exercise smoothly and effectively for five cycles sitting up, you may wish to try the more demanding version, which is done lying down. A bed, provided it's not too soft, or the floor can be used for this exercise. Lie down on your back, with a pillow placed so that your head and shoulders are slightly raised above the rest of your body. Again, breathe slowly and smoothly into your chest, hold the breath without closing your throat, and move the breath from chest to belly and back five times. Finish by breathing out. Repeat up to five times, and then relax your body completely on the final out breath, allowing every trace of muscular tension to flow away.

Without gravity to help you, it takes a great deal more control of your breathing muscles to move the breath down to the belly and back up to the chest without losing any through the throat. You'll probably be tempted to close your throat, rather than keeping the breath in your lungs by controlling your diaphragm and your chest muscles. Even apart from the possible damage to your lungs, though, closing your throat cheats you out of the extraordinary benefits of this exercise. Take your time, put up with the frustration of having to learn to do it right, and the effort will be repaid many times over. While learning it, you may find it useful to rest one hand on your chest and one on your belly, so that you can mre easily feel the movement of the breath up and down in your torso.

This exercise has a range of positive effects. First, by holding the breath and circulating it up and down through your torso, you maximize the amount of etheric energy your body absorbs from the air, as well as the exchange of gases in the bloodstream. Second, by expanding and contracting the chest, the diaphragm, and the abdominal wall, this exercise tones the muscles of the torso in ways that ordinary exercises cannot. Third, it massages the solar plexus—a large cluster of nerve cells, sometimes called the "abdominal brain," located in front of the spine at the level of the diaphragm. The solar plexus plays an important role in coordinating physical movement, and it is also associated with an important center of etheric energy in the body. The "internal massage" provided by this exercise releases excess tension, improves coordination, and helps increase and balance the flow of etheric energy.

Third breathing exercise:

This exercise lays the groundwork for the use of etheric energy in swordplay. Start by sitting in the same position as before, with your spine straight, your hands resting on your thighs, and your feet flat on the floor. Do several cycles of the Complete Breath as a warm up.

Next, as you breathe in and out, imagine that the breath is moving in and out through your feet, as though your legs were hollow tubes. Try to feel the air flowing in and out as you breathe, moving through the pores of your skin, passing through your legs and lower trunk to your lungs and out again the same way.

After a few cycles, redirect your breathing to your hands, and breathe in and out through them, as though your arms were hollow tubes. Go on to breathe through the knees; through the elbows; through knees and elbows together; through the hips; through the shoulders; through hips and shoulders together; through the abdomen; through the midriff, around the solar plexus; through the chest; through the head; and through the entire body, as though you were breathing in and out through every square inch of your skin. Each of these phases should be continued for several breaths.

It may take you a certain amount of imaginative effort to get the feeling of breath moving through the various parts of your body. The physical breath, obviously, doesn't travel anywhere outside the ordinary respiratory tract. What moves is etheric energy, which is extracted from the atmosphere by the subtle processes of breath, and can be sent at will anywhere in the body by the use of concentration and imagination. With practice, the sensation of moving air will become as solid as though the currents were actually air, as your body's etheric channels open to the flow of subtle energy.

This exercise should be practiced once or twice a day until you've learned to move the breath forcefully anywhere in your body you wish. At this point, it can be continued in the same way if you wish, or it can be done as a combined practice with the footwork training and the manual of the sword—the subjects of the next two chapters.

Fourth breathing exercise:

One further breathing exercise unfolds from the third one just described. To practice this exercise, draw your sword and take it in your sword hand, holding it in the standard grip covered in Chapter Two. Stand in a comfortable position, your back straight but not stiff; raise your sword arm close to horizontal, so that the sword is extended out in front of you.

Now, along the lines of the third breathing exercise, breathe in and out through the sword itself. Feel the air on the inbreath coming in through the blade, entering your hand through the hilt, flowing up your sword arm to your lungs; then, reversing the flow for the outbreath, let the air flow down your arm, into the hilt of the sword, along the blade and out into the surrounding air.

As you practice this exercise, you'll notice that you begin to feel the sword as though it was part of your own body, not simply a piece of metal held in your hand. This is one of the gifts of this exercise, and leads to steadily improving levels of dexterity and control, as well as to what sport fencers call the *sentiment de fer*—the "sense of steel," the capacity to "see" intuitively with the sword hand, which allows the skilled swordsman or swordswoman to anticipate and forestall the opponent's actions.

Two variations should be added to this exercise as soon as you've learned to breathe freely through the blade. The first is to do the same thing while moving the sword around, slowly at first, and then with increasing speed and force. The second is to draw in each inbreath through the forte of the sword—the half of the blade closest to the hilt—and to breathe out each outbreath through the foible—the half of the blade closest to the point. The forte is used to receive the opponent's cuts, while the foible is used to deliver cuts of your own; the relation between these rules of practice and the breathing pattern just described should not be hard to figure out.

Chapter Five
footwork training

The preparatory and breathing exercises presented in the last two chapters will help build a solid foundation for the training to come. In another sense, though, the foundation of swordsmanship is found in the hips, legs and feet. In order to prepare for swordplay, these parts of the body need to receive special strengthening and training for the work they will have to do.

It may seem strange that the lower half of the body should be so important in swordsmanship; after all, very few people hold a sword with their toes! Still, the sword in the hands of a competent swordsman or swordswoman is an extension of the body, and the root of all of the body's movements is its connection with the earth. Imagine for a moment that you were standing on a surface that offered no support or resistance to your movements—a sheet of smooth ice, for example, or a floor coated with a thick layer of oil. If you tried to take a step with one foot, the other would slip out from underneath you; if you tried to swing a sword, the movement would topple you off your feet. It would be impossible to do much of anything.

The same thing happens, in a somewhat subtler way, when someone with poorly developed legs and hips tries to make use of a sword. Without a firm foundation below the waist, it's impossible to handle a sword with any degree of finesse, because the movements of hand and arm in swordsmanship must always be an integral part of the dynamics of the entire body. On the most practical level, furthermore, footwork plays a crucial role in evading the opponent's attacks and carrying through your own.

Most people, even those who have well-developed lower bodies, lack the specific combination of strengths and skills needed for swordsmanship. Once again, though, there are exercises that will make up the difference. These should be learned and practiced only after you have worked with the preparatory exercises for several weeks at least, and it's a good idea to work on relaxation and get thoroughly comfortable with the first breathing exercise as well before you proceed to this next step on the path.

The Three Positions

To begin with, it's necessary to learn the three stances or, as they are called, positions, that are used in this system of swordsmanship. The positions are described here for those who are handling a sword with the right hand; if you are left-handed, or practicing with both hands, switch left and right in the following instructions.

Start by standing straight with your feet at right angles, the right foot pointing straight ahead, the left foot pointing to the left. The right heel is in front of the left heel, and touching it.

Your weight is mostly on the left foot, so that the right can move freely. This is first position.

Diagram 5-1

To move from first position to second, bend both knees out without moving the feet, lowering the body. The left knee should be above the toes of the left foot, and the right knee above those of the right foot, as shown in diagram 5-2. As you do this, shift the weight of your body entirely onto the left foot.

Diagram 5-2

Then, as a second motion, move the right foot straight ahead about eighteen inches—a little more or less depending on your height—and rest it there, the sole of the foot flat on the ground.

All your weight remains on the left foot, so that you can lift your left foot up off the ground without shifting your balance or changing your position at all. (Try it and see.) This is second position.

Diagram 5-3

To move from second position to third, step forward another eighteen inches or so with the right foot, shifting the weight forward onto the right foot and straightening the left leg without locking the knee. This is third position.

Diagram 5-4

In actual combat, first position is used when parrying or evading an opponent's attacks; second position is used when moving into range, when first engaging, or in the intervals between attacks and parries; and third position is used for making attacks. If you have any background in the Asian martial arts, you'll have noticed that second position is similar to what karate practitioners call the "cat stance," while third position has a good deal in common with karate's "bow stance." Although there's no evidence that these similarities are a result of borrowing, they aren't accidental. In combat, what works in China or Okinawa generally also works in England or North America, and similar situations tend to give rise to similar responses.

Footwork Exercises

In some Asian martial arts, it's common to have students stand in postures such as the horse stance for extended periods, as a way of building lower-body strength. The approach used in Western swordsmanship is somewhat different. The three positions are not meant to be used as static poses, but rather as phases of motion through which the swordsman or swordswoman moves in combat. The footwork exercises, therefore, are patterns of movement from position to position.

In learning footwork, it's necessary to avoid the common bad habit of adjusting the upper body to make up for poor lower-body strength and position. In order to prevent this, while doing these exercises, cross your arms behind your back and grasp each arm below the elbow with the opposite hand. This holds your shoulders in a stable position and straightens the spine; it also focuses attention on the muscles of your back. (Try walking around a little with your arms held this way, and see what you notice.) This should be done in all the following footwork exercises.

First footwork exercise:

This exercise teaches the most basic of these patterns of movement. Begin by folding your arms behind your back as just described, and then take first position. Then, just as described above, move from first to second position. (Be sure to do this in two distinct motions: first, bending the knees out, without moving the feet; second, stepping ahead with the right foot.) Then, as described above, move from second to third position, stepping further forward with the right foot and shifting your weight forward onto it.

Now reverse the process, shifting your weight back onto your left foot and bringing the right foot back, until you have returned to second position. At this point, tap your right foot twice on the floor, hard enough that you can hear two distinct raps. This is called a double appel. In combat, a single or double appel—that is, one or two raps made with the foot—can be used to distract the opponent briefly, while making an attack or a counter. In free practice between partners, the appel is used as a signal that the swordsman or swordswoman who makes it is ready to begin combat. In footwork training, on the other hand, the double appel forces you to shift your weight all the way back onto your left foot, thus ensuring a clean movement from third to second position.

Finally, move back from second to first position. Again, this is done in two distinct stages, first bringing the right foot back against the left one, knees out, then straightening the knees and rising up into first position. Then repeat the entire exercise, going from first position to second and then to third, and from third to second and then to first, and continue.

This first footwork exercise is the most important of all, and it should be done relentlessly if you intend to master the way of the sword. Your goal is to be able to move from position to position quickly and dextrously, with a feeling of lightness but with a firm connection to the ground.

Depending on your physical condition, you may need to start off with only a few repetitions, and if your knees are weak you may have to take a day or two off between sessions to allow the muscles, tendons and ligaments to get used to the unfamiliar effort. If your legs hurt at the end of a session, wait until the pain is gone before you do another one, so that any potential damage can be healed. If your condition permits, though, this footwork exercise should be done daily, and the number of repetitions should increase step by step until you can do fifty or more without the least difficulty or discomfort.

Second footwork exercise:

The second exercise is a development of the first, and duplicates the shifts of weight and position that occur most often in actual combat. Start by crossing the arms behind the back, as in the first exercise, and then take up first position. Next, lower the body, bending the knees outward, exactly as though you were going to go to second position, and then step forward thirty-six inches and take third position. Step back, returning to the posture with feet together and knees out, and then straighten your knees and return to first position.

Repeat, going from first position directly to third and from third back to first. Again, although you should be careful to start out with a level of practice that won't strain or injure your body, the goal to aim for is one session of this exercise every day, fifty repetitions or more, without difficulty or discomfort.

Third footwork exercise:

The third exercise is designed to develop strength and poise in the lower body. Start by crossing the arms behind the back, as before, and take first position. Then, exactly as described in the first footwork exercise, move to second position. At this point, without shifting your body weight, lift your right foot from the ground and move it back, touching the right toes to the ground about eight inches behind the left heel, as shown in diagram 5-6.

Diagram 5-6

At this point, leaving the feet where they are, straighten the left knee, so that the body rises up. Once it is straight, bend it again, and then move the right foot forward and return to second position. Repeat from second position. Again, your goal should be to practice this exercise daily, though you should start out with a schedule of practice that doesn't cause pain; fifty repetitions without difficulty is a good target to aim for over the long run.

Another dimension can be added to all these exercises by combining them with the third breathwork exercise given in Chapter Four. To do this, you'll need to coordinate breathing with movement. The essential rule here is to breathe out when stepping forward or lowering the body, and to breathe in when drawing back or raising the body.

Practice this for a few sessions, until it comes automatically. Then begin breathing through different parts of the body, just as in the third breathing exercise, as you do the footwork exercises. Concentrate on learning to breathe through the legs, feet, and hips, since these are the parts of the body you're using most in these exercises. It can also be useful, though, to explore breathing through other parts of your body while doing footwork exercises. Eventually, if you continue with this phase of training, the currents of etheric energy will be constantly spiraling in and out through different parts of your body as you respond to the demands of combat. The more you can move toward this sort of freely moving balance of energies in the early part of your training, the better.

Footwork In Combat

The basic methods of moving from place to place used in this system of swordsmanship are the advance, the retreat, and the traverse. In order to learn them, begin as before, by crossing the arms behind the back; take first position, then move into second position in the way already described.

To advance, from second position, move the right foot about fifteen inches forward. Shift the body weight onto it just long enough to bring the left foot fifteen inches forward, and then settle the weight back on the left foot, resuming second position. Repeat.

Diagram 5-7

To retreat, from second position, shift the weight forward, and step back about fifteen inches with the left foot. As soon as the left foot has settled into place, shift the weight back onto it and draw the right foot back about fifteen inches correspondingly, resuming second position. Repeat.

Diagram 5-8

To traverse to the right, from second position, move the right foot about twelve inches to the right, and shift the weight onto it just long enough to bring the left foot twelve inches to the right after it. Settle the weight back on the left foot, resuming second position. Repeat.

To traverse to the left, from second position, shift the weight forward, and move the left foot about twelve inches to the left. As soon as it has settled in place, shift the weight back onto it, and move the right foot about twelve inches to the left, resuming second position. Repeat.

Diagram 5-9

These are the foundations of footwork in swordsmanship, but in some cases it's necessary to cover ground more quickly. The additional methods used here are the step, the pass, and the stride.

To step forward, from second position, shift the weight forward, onto the right foot. Bring the left foot forward until it touches the heel of the right foot, just as in first position. Do not straighten the knees, however. As soon as the left foot is in position, shift the weight onto it and step forward with the right foot, resuming second position. Repeat.

Diagram 5-10

To step backward, from second position, draw your right foot back until its heel touches the left foot, just as in first position. Do not straighten the knees. Instead, as soon as the right foot is in position, shift the weight onto it and step back with the left foot. Shift the weight backwards onto the left foot, resuming second position. Repeat.

Diagram 5-11

To pass forward, from second position, shift the weight forward onto the right foot. Bring the left foot forward past the right foot, and set it down about twelve inches ahead of the right foot, with its toes pointing to the left. Shift the weight onto the left foot, and step forward at once with the right foot, resuming second position. Repeat.

Diagram 5-12

To pass backward, from second position, draw the right foot back behind the left foot and set it down, toes pointing forward, about twelve inches behind the left foot. Shift the weight onto the right foot, and step back at once with the left foot. Shift the weight back onto the left foot, resuming second position. Repeat.

Diagram 5-13

To stride right, throw your right foot as far as possible to the right and shift the weight onto it, bending the right knee. The toes of the right foot face toward the right, while the left toes pivot to face forward, so that the result looks like a sideways third position. This is used to move suddenly to one side, to avoid a sudden charge or an attack that can't readily be parried. Depending on the opponent's actions, you can proceed from this point either by shifting the weight back to your left foot and returning to your original position, or by using a volte (described below) to pivot around and face the opponent, drawing your left leg out of harm's way, and resuming second position.

Diagram 5-14

To stride left, shift the weight forward, and immediately throw your left foot as far as possible to the left, setting it down with the toes pointing toward the left and shifting your weight onto it, so that the result looks like a sideways third position. From here, again, you can either return to your original position, or simply step after with the right foot, resuming second position.

Diagram 5-15

A final detail of footwork is the volte, which is used to pivot suddenly to one side or to the rear. It is used when you are faced with attack from an unexpected quarter, and in other situations where it's useful to be facing a different direction very quickly.

To volte, shift the weight forward onto your right foot, and then step with the left foot, either to the left, to the right, or straight ahead. Put the left foot down, shift the weight onto it, and then pivot on the ball of the right foot to face away from the left foot, toward the new direction, resuming second position. (Note that the direction you'll be facing is the opposite of that in which the left foot steps.) Repeat.

Diagram 5-16

Like the other aspects of footwork training, all these patterns of movement need to be practiced systematically, so that you can move forward, backward and to either side without having to think about what you're doing. (To maximize this aspect of the training, once you can do the footwork methods quickly and efficiently on a smooth floor, try them outdoors on rough ground, in a variety of environments.) The ways of moving given here keep the body covered as far as possible against any attack the opponent may make while you are moving; still, this won't do you much good if the process of moving in the right way distracts you at the wrong moment. Here as elsewhere, regular practice is the master key.

Chapter Six
the manual of the sword

Once the preparatory exercises have been learned and practiced for several weeks, you'll be ready to take up the sword itself and begin learning how to use it. The first step in this process is a set of individual exercises traditionally called "the manual of the sword." This sounds like a book, but a manual of the sword in the old sense of the term is actually a solo practice form including all the fundamental techniques of swordsmanship; in function, if not in form, it's somewhat similar to the katas used in karate and other Asian martial arts.

The manual of the sword is the heart of the tradition of swordsmanship taught here; everything in the previous chapters feeds into it, in one way or another, and everything in the chapters to come follows out of it. The time you take to learn it and master it will not be wasted.

Preparation For The Manual

All the movements in the manual are to be done with a real sword. This is essential in teaching the student to handle live steel, but it poses certain requirements—after all, a sword can do nearly as much damage to furniture and wallpaper as it can to a human body. You'll need to find a space, indoors or outdoors, where you can move the sword around yourself freely without putting anything around you at risk.

The first step in practicing the manual, then, is to pick up the sword, put yourself in the proper position, and then make sure that you have enough room to practice.

Starting position:

Start by standing in first position, with the sword in your right hand. (If you're left-handed with a sword, or practicing with your left hand as suggested earlier, you'll need to reverse left and right in all of the following instructions.) For now, leave your sword hand at your side and rest the point of the sword on the ground a little in front of your right toes.

The position of your left arm is of some importance. Tuck your left arm behind your back, the lower arm parallel to your belt, the elbow above your left hip and the hand, which is closed into a fist, above your right hip. This is the standard position for practice of all kinds, as it keeps the hand out of harm's way and also teaches the student to keep the shoulders square and to use the momentum of the whole body in cuts and thrusts.

In the old texts, opinion was divided as to whether this position of the left arm should actually be used in life-or-death combat. Some sources present it as the standard combat posture; others urge the student to keep the left hand in front of the body, and to be ready to use it to knock thrusts aside, seize the opponent's hilt in close-in fighting, throw stones or other objects at the opponent, and so on.

Diagram 6-3   Diagram 6-3

The carry:

From the basic position just described, with a movement of your hand and wrist, bring the sword up in an arc until the back rests against your right shoulder. Allow your grip to shift until you are holding the hilt the way you hold a pen, with the grip between the thumb and forefinger and the other three fingers tucked behind it. This position is called the "carry," and is used at the beginning and end of the manual of the sword.

Diagram 6-3

Prove distance:

Now resume an ordinary grip on the hilt as you extend the sword and sword arm straight out to the right, to their maximum reach. Make sure that there's nothing within striking range to that side. Return to the carry, and then extend the sword and sword arm to their full extension to the left, resuming the ordinary grip, turning your upper body as far to the left as it will go without moving your feet or changing the position of your left arm. Again, make sure that there's nothing within striking range to that side, and then return to the carry. Finally, extend the sword and sword arm straight out in front of you, as though you were executing a thrust against an opponent. Once again, make sure that nothing is close enough to be hit, and then return to first position and resume the carry. At this point, you're ready to begin practice.

The Seven Cuts

There are traditionally seven cuts, which correspond to the seven guards or defensive movements. The first part of the manual of the sword is devoted to teaching the student how these are done.

For the early stages of training, it can be useful to have a target—a circle around 36 inches in diameter, made of wood or heavy poster board, which can be mounted on a wall or supported by a post. It has seven lines marked on it, all converging at the center, as shown in diagram 6-4. It should be positioned in front of the student, out of sword range, with the central point at the level of the heart.

In practicing the first section of the manual, the student should try to make his or her cuts follow the lines on the target; this helps develop precision and dexterity in handling the sword, and helps make sure the cuts are aimed as they should be. It should be understood, though, that these seven are not the only angles at which a cut can be directed—they are simply a convenience for training, and can be varied at will according to the circumstances of actual combat.

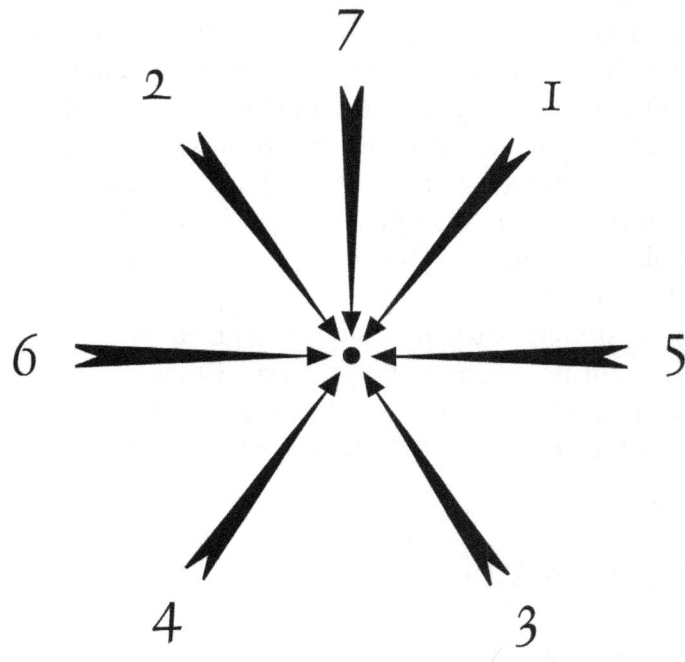

Diagram 6-4

Throughout the manual, the student remains in first position, and allows the movements to follow the full arc of their momentum. Like the seven lines on the target, these habits are also conveniences for training, rather than rules for combat; they allow the student to focus on the movements of the arm and hand in isolation, and teach the somewhat complex dynamics of handling a sword effectively. In actual combat, the swordsman or swordswoman shifts constantly between positions, and any cut that misses its target or is parried is instantly converted into a new movement—but all this requires a good deal of training before it can be done competently.

Preparation for cuts:

Take up first position, with the sword at the carry and the left arm tucked behind your back as before, the target in front of you and plenty of room in all directions. Prove distance if you haven't already done so. Then bring the point of the sword up and back, resting the back of the blade on your shoulder, until the blade is horizontal, with the point extending back behind you and the edge turned slightly out to the right. Grasp the hilt in the correct manner, with the thumb on the back of the hilt. Your grip should be firm but flexible, allowing a certain amount of play to the hilt.

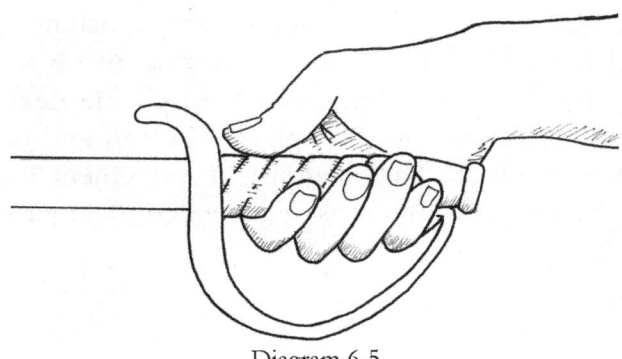
Diagram 6-5

Cut one:

Push the hilt straight forward, as though you were throwing the pommel of the sword straight at an opponent's face. Keep the blade of the sword pointed straight behind you as long as you can. At a certain point, which will vary based on the strength and flexibility of your wrists, the sword will naturally arc up and out.

At this point, allow the blade to move in a diagonal arc to the upper right, and then down toward the center, following line 1 on the target. As the sword arcs up, draw your wrist back and down, so that your arm reaches full extension well before the point of the sword comes opposite the center of the target. The entire movement is a little like cracking a whip; this is one of the most important details of the entire practice, as it focuses the energy of the entire body into the cut, and helps the blade cut with maximum efficiency.

Let the point of the sword sweep past the center of the target until it is in front of your left hip—remember, you are cutting through the circle defined by the target, not simply touching it—and then allow the wrist to pivot and the hand to turn over, letting the blade follow through the rest of its arc to the lower left and then up. Finish the movement with the point behind your left shoulder, the blade parallel to the ground, the edge turned a little out to the left, and the right hand above and in front of your left shoulder, ready for the next cut.

In the early phases of training, it's best to make each cut slowly, and to divide it into four phases—pushing out the hilt, snapping around with the blade, allowing the blade to follow through, and bringing hand and sword to the next position—concentrating on making each phase as clean and exact as possible. Later, once the basic pattern of movement has been well learned, the four phases should be blended together into a single movement.

Diagram 6-6

Cut two:

Again, push the hilt straight forward, allowing the blade to snap around in a diagonal arc along line 2 of the target. The arm reaches full extension and begins to withdraw before the point comes opposite the target's center, with the same whiplike snap. Allow the blade to follow through with its arc of motion. The blade comes to rest at your lower right, pointing diagonally downward; as it descends, turn the wrist so that the edge is forward, and allow the point to move slightly behind you.

Diagram 6-7

Cut three:

This is the most difficult of the seven cuts to execute cleanly and strongly. Move your sword hand and the hilt of the sword up from the lower right, allowing the blade to fall behind, and then let the blade arc forward as the hilt comes opposite the target's center, cutting up along line 3 with the usual whiplike snapping motion. Allow the blade to follow through until the point falls back behind you, turning your wrist over as it does so. Finish the cut with your sword hand level with your left elbow, the blade pointing up and the edge back.

Diagram 6-8

Cut four:

Push the hilt forward toward the center of the target, bringing the blade in an arc down, forward and up diagonally from the lower left along line 4. As before, your arm reaches full extension and begins to move toward the next starting position before the point reaches the center of the target. Let the point go past the target until it is in front of your right shoulder, then allow your wrist to turn over to let the blade follow through. Finish with your sword hand near your right shoulder, your right elbow low, the blade parallel to the ground, the point extended behind your left shoulder, and the edge facing back.

Diagram 6-9

Cut five:

Push the hilt straight forward, and bring the blade snapping out in a horizontal arc, using the same whiplike motion as before. Bring the point past the center of the target until it is in front of your left shoulder, and then turn the wrist over and allow the sword to follow through, finishing with the sword hand near the left shoulder, the blade parallel to the ground, the point extended to your right, the edge facing back.

Diagram 6-10

Cut six:

Push the hilt straight forward as before and follow with the blade, cutting horizontally along line 6 of the target with the same snapping and drawing motion as before. Bring the point past the target's center until it is in front of your right shoulder, and then turn your wrist over to allow the blade to follow through. Then raise your sword hand up above your head, finishing with the blade extended back, point down slightly, edge facing up.

Diagram 6-11

Cut seven:

Push the hilt straight forward and follow with the blade as before, cutting straight down along line 7 to the center of the target, and then stop the sword in that position. (This serves as a way to check your handling of the sword; if you can't stop it cleanly and precisely, you need to work on control and, possibly, on the strength of your grip.)

Diagram 6-12

The Three Thrusts

In the days when swords were among the most common means of personal defense, nearly all systems of swordsmanship used both cuts and thrusts. This balance was broken in the early modern period; rapier and smallsword fencing systems using only thrusts came to dominate the specialized field of the formal duel, while many systems of military swordsmanship came to depend on cuts alone. Loud disputes over the relative merits of thrusting and cutting have been going on ever since, generating a good deal more heat than light.

The entire debate can be set aside for our purposes, though, since it's clear—whether thrusts or cuts are "better" in some abstract sense—that a swordsman or swordswoman who knows how to make both and defend against both will be in a stronger position than one who can only do one or the other. Most eighteenth- and nineteenth-century systems of swordsmanship, including the one presented in this book, took this eminently sensible viewpoint, and most of the standard manuals of the sword thus included both types of attack.

The second section of the manual of the sword, therefore, teaches the three thrusts. The movements involved may seem a little unusual at first, but they produce thrusts that are more efficient and less easily parried than the sort of naive straight thrust made by untrained swordsmen. The starting position for this section of the manual is the same one in which you finished the last movement of the first section.

Thrust one:

From the final position of cut seven, bring the hilt of the sword down and across your body until it is in front of your left hip, with the sword hand turned palm up, the blade slanting slightly upwards, and the edge of the sword toward the left. Then thrust forward with the point, raising your sword hand to the level of the left shoulder and turning it slightly, so that the edge of the sword faces diagonally up and to the left. The point rises slightly and then descends to the center of the target, and the blade slants down and in. Finally, draw the sword back along the same line of motion, bringing the hand back to a position in front of the left hip.

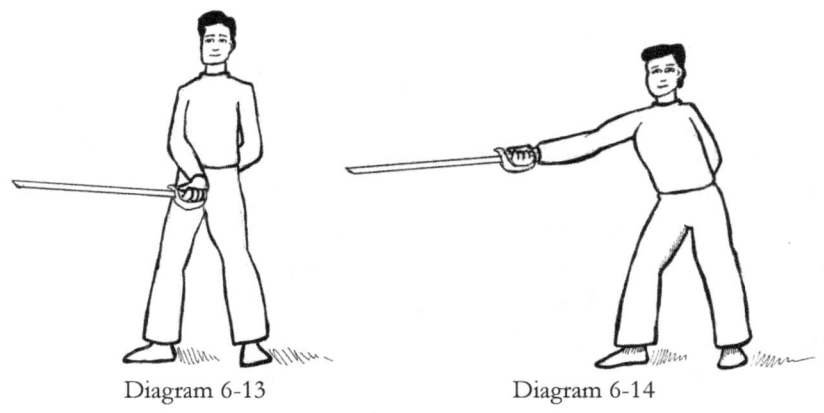

Diagram 6-13   Diagram 6-14

The critical detail to be learned and practiced here, and with all of the thrusts, is the movement of the point in a shallow arc. A straight thrust is relatively easy to parry, but a thrust that follows a curve can go around an incautious parry to strike home.

Thrust two:

From the final position of thrust one, bring the hand across the body and up until it is above and in front of the right shoulder, turning the hand so the palm faces out and the edge faces upwards, and directing the point straight ahead. Then thrust forward, allowing the point to descend in an arc toward the center of the target. Finish the thrust with the edge still turned upwards, the sword hand in front of the right shoulder, and the blade angling down toward the center. Finally, draw the sword back along the same line of motion to the position from which the thrust started, with the right hand above the level of the shoulder.

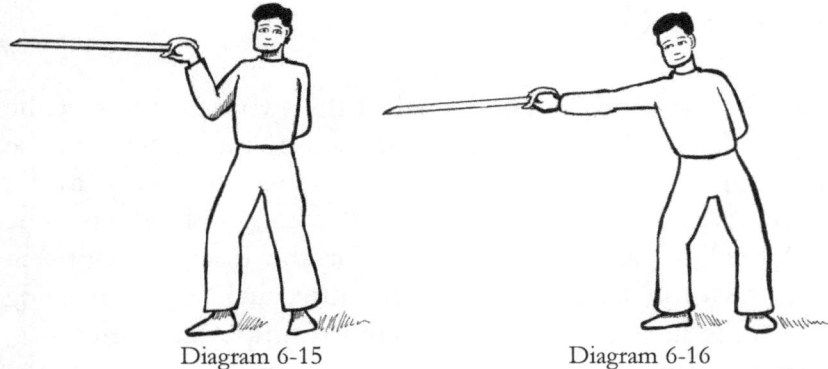

Diagram 6-15   Diagram 6-16

Thrust three:

From the final position of thrust two, bring the sword hand down, positioning it in front of the right hip with the palm up and the edge of the sword facing upwards. The blade is angled upward, with the point rising to the level of the heart. Thrust forward with the point, raising the sword hand to the level of the right shoulder, and allowing the point to rise and then fall along a shalow arc on its way to the center of the target. Finish with the edge of the sword still turned upwards, and the blade slanting gently downwards toward the point. Finally, draw back the sword along the same line of motion, returning your sword hand in front of the right hip.

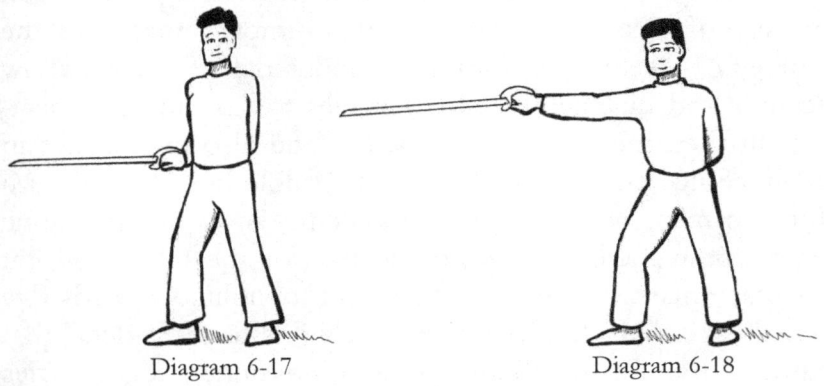

Diagram 6-17   Diagram 6-18

The Seven Guards

The third section of the manual of the sword consists of the seven guards, which protect against the seven cuts. These are the basic defensive movements of the system, and need to be practiced at least as systematically as the cuts and thrusts. The word "guard" is also used at times for the basic positions in which the sword is held between techniques, such as the engaging guard and the hanging guard, but there's an important difference. The seven defensive guards described here are dynamic patterns of movement, not static postures; to hold one of these guards statically is to leave yourself vulnerable to attack.

An important detail about defensive moves needs to be addressed here as well. Many modern books about swordsmanship insist that guards and parries should always be executed with the flat of the blade. This appears to have been standard practice in the Middle Ages and in many Renaissance combat systems, but by the eighteenth century, matters had changed. The standard military handbooks of swordsmanship in the nineteenth and early twentieth centuries taught parrying with the edge, not the flat. Since many of these books were written by men who had defended their lives at swords' points, an experience few modern writers can claim, their advice can't simply be dismissed out of hand.

The difference in approach was made possible by changes in the quality of steel in recent centuries—improvements in the technology of steelmaking during the industrial revolution allow eighteenth- and nineteenth-century blades to take more punishment than their medieval counterparts—and also by changes in technique. Since cuts are made with the foible but blocked with the forte in most post-Renaissance systems, an edge parry done correctly doesn't risk damage to the part of the blade you cut with. In fact, many of the nineteenth-century military swords I've examined have sharp foibles but relatively dull fortes, a detail that strengthens the forte's ability to hold up under edge parries without taking significant damage.

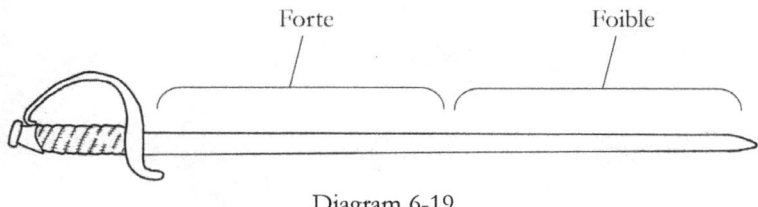

Diagram 6-19

The value of parrying with the edge comes from the additional strength it allows you to put into your parries. Your grip is strongest against impacts against the sword's edge, whether those come from hitting an opposing sword or an opponent's body. Turning the edge of your blade against the opponent's cut also involves a twisting motion of the wrist. This is an important element of the technique, and it's one of the places where having your thumb along the back of the hilt makes the most difference.

With practice, you'll find that it's possible to make the parry with a sudden, snapping motion that imparts a good deal of momentum to your sword all at once. This allows you to counter the momentum of the opponent's sword effectively and keep a cut from pushing through your guard.

Guard one:

From the position in which you ended the last technique of the second section, straighten your wrist, turning the edge down. Then bring the hilt of the sword across to the left, until it is positioned to the left and in front of your left shoulder. The point of the sword angles forward and in toward the center, and the edge turns outward to the left with a twisting motion of the wrist. Your grip is somewhat tighter than when cutting.

Diagram 6-20

Guard two:

From guard one, carry the hilt back across to the right until it is outside and in front of the right shoulder, with the point sloping forward and toward the center. Twist the edge out to the right. Your elbow should be close to your side.

Diagram 6-21

Guard three:

From guard two, lower the sword hand and allow the point to descend, turning the wrist so that the fingernails are facing up. Bring the hilt across the body until it is in front of the left hip. The sword's edge is toward the left, and the blade slants forward and toward the middle, so that the point is in front of the right leg.

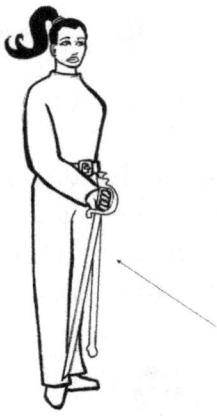

Diagram 6-22

Guard four:

From guard three, turn the hand over and carry it to the right until it is outside and in front of the right hip. The edge of the sword is to the right, and the blade is angled forward and toward the middle, so that the point is again in front of the right leg.

Diagram 6-23

Guard five:

From guard four, raise the hand to shoulder height and carry it across the body to the left until it is about six inches past the left shoulder. The blade is held vertically, point downwards, with the edge turned outwards to the left.

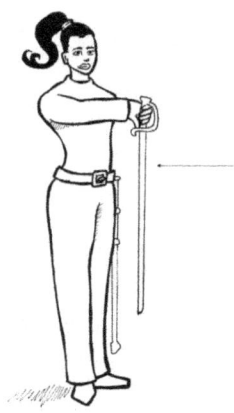

Diagram 6-24

Guard six:

From guard five, carry the hand across at shoulder level to the right, drawing the shoulder and elbow back so that the elbow does not go past the protection of the blade. The blade is held vertically, six inches out from the shoulder; the point is directed downwards, and the edge is turned outwards to the right.

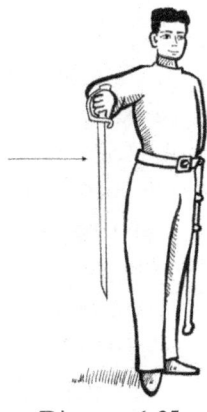

Diagram 6-25

Guard seven:

From guard six, raise the hand well above the head and move it forward until it is well in front of the elbow, with the palm facing to the right. The right shoulder is pulled a little back. The blade slants down, forward and to the left, with the edge up and the point on a level with the left shoulder.

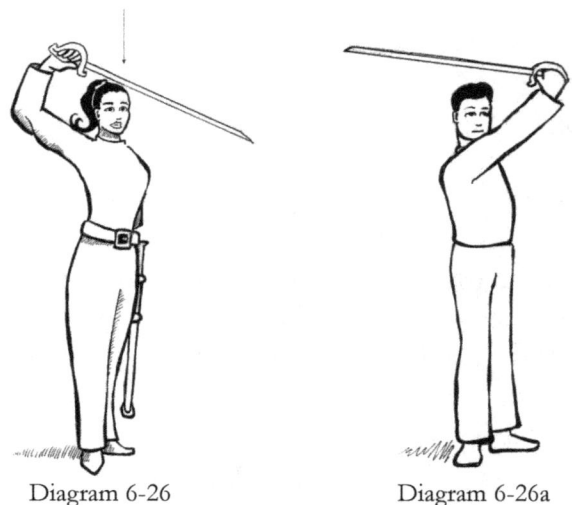

Diagram 6-26   Diagram 6-26a

An alternative version of guard seven, called the St. George guard, is well worth learning. (See Diagram 6-26a). From guard seven, bring the hand and arm across to the left, turning the hand over, so the palm is up. The sword slants across to the right and down. The difference between guard seven and the St. George guard is offensive, not defensive; both protect equally well against a cut seven, but you can move from guard seven at once into cuts one, three, or five, while the St. George guard leads just as instantly into cuts two, four, or six. Switching from one to the other in combat can catch an opponent unprepared.

Parries And Moulinets

The fourth section of the manual of the sword consist of the three parries, followed by moulinets. These are sweeping, circular motions used to deflect thrusting attacks. To a certain degree, the three parries correspond to the three thrusts just as the guards correspond to the cuts, but the comparison is not exact. The parries are rarely used against sword thrusts; instead, they are meant for use against heavier thrusting weapons such as spears, bayonets, and boarding pikes. Your starting position is guard seven.

Parry one:

Lower the sword hand to a position in front of the right shoulder, bringing the point up and turning the edge to the right. Then, with a movement of the wrist, bring the point quickly up, around, and back behind you, turning the wrist over so that the blade executes a full circle to the right side of your body, finishing with the blade slanting upwards and the edge facing toward the left.

Diagram 6-27

Parry two:

With the hand remaining at the level of the right shoulder, bring the point up, around and down to your left side, executing a full circle on that side of your body. Finish with the blade pointing straight upward, edge to the right.

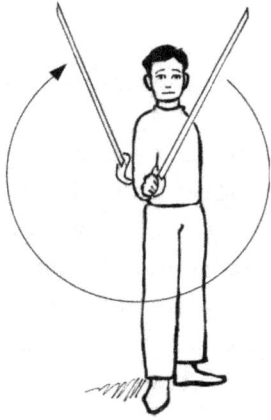

Diagram 6-28

Parry three:

From this position, bring the point down to the left in a half-circle in front of the body, so that the back of the sword sweeps down and outward. Finish with the sword some six inches out from the body to the right, the point straight down, the edge to the left, and the sword hand still at the level of the right shoulder.

Diagram 6-29

Moulinets:

From parry three, bring the blade back up along the same arc until it is upright, with the edge to the right. Execute parry one and then, without stopping or slowing the sword in its path, go on to execute parry two. Stop at the conclusion of parry two, and turn your wrist so that the edge of the blade faces left. Then execute parry two again, and without stopping or slowing the blade, go on to parry one. Finally, return to the engaging guard, and then to the carry, to finish the manual.

Moulinets can be done continuously as well—parry one followed by parry two followed by parry one and so forth, without pause—so that the sword weaves a cocoon of steel around the swordsman or swordswoman. This was considered to be an excellent way to make the wrist of the sword hand strong and flexible, and was also highly regarded as a defense against spear or bayonet thrusts if done skillfully.

Mastering The Manual

The four sections above include all the basic techniques of the sword, and once they are learned, these fundamentals of swordsmanship simply need to be woven into patterns of effective combat. For this very reason, though, the manual must be studied and practiced carefully, systematically, and relentlessly. Every movement must become second nature, so that you can do any of them instantly, with swiftness, poise, and precision.

If you have the time and the stamina to do so, practicing the manual multiple times every day—along with the basic exercises, breathing exercises and footwork—will enable you to master the fundamentals of swordsmanship in the shortest possible time. If time, circumstances, or your physical condition don't permit, do the manual as often as you can. Less than twice a week will make for long delays in learning, as your body will forget most of the wordless lessons it learns from one session of practice by the time the next one comes around. Still, it's better to practice it as often as you can—even if that's once a week, or even less—than to do nothing at all. When you do practice, it's best to do the manual as many times in succession as you can do efficiently and with good form. Stop before your muscles become so tired that your technique gets sloppy.

In the early phases of training, it's best to do the techniques of the manual slowly, with concentration and focus, making the motions as precise and clear and possible. Techniques such as cuts, which include several different stages of motion, should be divided up into phases which are practiced one at a time. It can be tempting to focus on speed too soon, but this leads to poor technique and inept swordplay. Pay attention to what you are doing, and don't let yourself be fooled into thinking that speed can make up for incompetent form.

When you have mastered the details of the techniques, pay attention to the interface between movement and breath. Concentrate on breathing out as you make a cut, thrust, guard or parry, and breathing in as you follow through and get into position for the next one. Then, once this becomes second nature, try to "breathe into" each movement, feeling the etheric energy of the outbreath flowing out the sword arm and along the sword as you make each outward movement, along the lines of the third breathing exercise from Chapter Four. Let the flow of energy reach the tip of the sword as the movement reaches its full extension. As you draw back, let the energy flow back inward accordingly. This coordinates the subtle energies of the body and leads to levels of skill that a purely muscular approach to swordsmanship can't reach.

Finally, when form and breath have been integrated into the practice of the manual, begin to work on speed and flow. Lightness, not muscular effort, is the key factor here. Focus on making the movements of the manual a single unbroken motion; pay attention to your body as you move, and let go of excess tension. Move as fast as you can without breaking the flow, and you'll find that each time you move a little faster. Given steady and systematic practice, you'll achieve a degree of quickness that would have astounded you in the beginning.

A common error is to try to force speed by pushing the muscles harder, trying to achieve speed by strength. This interferes with the precision needed for effective swordplay, and increases muscle tension, making your movements ponderous and jerky. While quickness is of vital importance in swordsmanship, it's important to pursue it in the right way! Do the manual lightly, fluidly, and precisely, with your body in the golden mean of balance—neither tense nor limp, but poised—and speed will take care of itself.

Two subtle variations of speed are important in the techniques of the manual; one is used for guards and parries, the other for cuts and thrusts. Attacking techniques should be made with maximum speed from the very beginning, like a bullet from a gun. This makes them harder to intercept or anticipate. Defensive moves, on the other hand, should accelerate as they go, so that they reach full force just as they come to their final position. This makes it easier to redirect a guard or parry if the opponent's attack changes unexpectedly.

Chapter Seven
attack and defense

The manual of the sword teaches all the basic techniques of swordsmanship—the cuts, thrusts, guards and parries that make up the alphabet of combat. Just as the alphabet has to be learned before it's possible to begin reading even the simplest sentence, the manual must be learned, practiced systematically, and committed to memory before going further.

When you will be ready to start the next stage of training will depend on a range of factors. People learn at different rates, depending on individual talents and abilities, and on the amount of time and effort devoted to training. For most people, though, several weeks of daily practice of the manual is a bare minimum. Until you can do the entire manual from memory, with form, breath and speed integrated in each movement, you'll be better off working on the manual alone for the time being.

Combining Attack And Defense

Assuming that you've learned the manual thoroughly, the next step is to start weaving together the techniques of the manual with footwork, to begin making the transition from the formal patterns of the manual to the realities of combat. The following exercise, like the manual, should be done with a real sword. There are two starting positions for the exercise, corresponding to the two basic postures used in combat: the engaging guard and the hanging guard.

The engaging guard:

Take up first position, come to the carry, and then prove distance, just as in the opening movements of the manual. Then move into second position, and bring your sword hand forward and up to the level of your solar plexus, about eighteen inches in front of your body. As the sword leaves the carry, take the hilt in the standard grasp, the four fingers lightly but firmly around the grip, the thumb along the back. The point of the sword should be at the level of the top of your head, with the blade leaning neither to the left nor to the right, and the edge facing forward. Your left hand is tucked behind your back, just as in the manual. This posture is called the engaging guard, and it's the most common posture used when you first cross blades with an opponent.

Diagram 7-1

The hanging guard:

An alternative posture, called the hanging guard, should also be learned and practiced, as it's more useful in some situations. To take up the hanging guard, begin exactly as described above, entering first position, proving distance and moving into second position. Instead of bringing your sword hand to solar plexus level, though, raise it up above the level of your head, between twelve and eighteen inches in front of your forehead, with the blade slanting down, forward, and to your left side.

Diagram 6-29

This is a more aggressive posture than the engaging guard, since almost any movement of the arm from this position can be developed instantly into a powerful cut. The engaging guard is slightly better positioned for defensive moves, especially against cuts to the leg and the right side. Each has its place. In learning and practicing the following exercises, it's best to start out with the engaging guard, but at a later stage of practice the same patterns of movement can and should be done with the hanging guard as a starting point.

First cut and guard:

To begin the exercise, from the engaging guard, move forward quickly into third position. As you do so, thrust your sword hand forward, letting the point come back, and execute cut one toward the left side of an imaginary opponent's head. As the cut reaches full extension, spring back to first position and bring the sword straight back into guard one, as though the opponent was making cut one against you. In all these parries, remember to position the parry as though you were catching the cut on the forte of your blade.

Second cut and guard:

From guard one, move forward again into third Position. Again, as you move, thrust your sword hand forward and let the point fall behind slightly, and execute cut two toward the right side of the imaginary opponent's head. As soon as the cut reaches full extension, spring back to first position and bring the blade up and back into guard two, as though the opponent was making cut two against you.

Third cut and guard:

From guard two, go forward again into third position, while allowing the point of the sword to fall back behind your right shoulder in a circular movement on your right. Bring the blade around, forward and up, executing cut three toward the underside of the opponent's wrist. As the cut reaches full extension, spring back to first position, lower the point and bring the blade across to your left into guard three, as though the opponent was making cut three against you.

Fourth cut and guard:

In the same way, go forward to third position, meanwhile bringing the point up, back and around in a circular motion on your left, then executing cut four toward the opponent's forward leg. As soon as the cut reaches full extension, spring back to first position, drop the point and move your sword hand to the right to make guard four, as though the opponent was making cut four against you.

Fifth cut and guard:

Go forward into third position, meanwhile raising your sword hand above the level of your head and moving the blade into a horizontal position, point to the left and edge to the rear. Thrust your sword hand forward and snap the blade around, executing cut five against the left side of the opponent's head, neck or body. As soon as the cut reaches full extension, spring back to first position, drop the point, bring the sword across your body to your left, and turn the wrist to make guard five, as though the opponent was making cut five against you.

Sixth cut and guard:

Go forward into third position, bringing the point up behind you, thrusting your sword hand forward, and executing cut six against the right side of the opponent's head, neck or body. As soon as the cut reaches full extension, spring back to first position, drop the point and bring the hilt to the right of your body, making guard six, as though the opponent was making cut six against you.

Seventh cut and guard:

Go forward again into third position, raising the forearm of your sword arm over your head and bringing the sword around past your left shoulder, point staying low, until the blade is behind your head and shoulders, angling downwards, edge to the back. Execute cut seven toward the top of the opponent's head. As soon as the cut reaches full extension, spring back into first position, turning your wrist so that the edge of the sword faces up, and raising your hand to make guard seven, as though the opponent was making cut seven against you.

First thrust and parry:

Again, move forward into third position. Meanwhile, lower the sword hand to a position in front of the left hip, turn the point forward, and execute thrust one. As soon as the thrust has reached full extension, draw the blade back along the same path as you spring back into first position, and bring the point of the sword up, with the edge to the right. Perform parry one, as though parrying a thrust from your opponent.

Second thrust and parry:

Finishing parry one, your sword hand is in front of your right shoulder, with the blade slanting upwards and the edge to your left. Step forward into third position, bringing your hand up across your body until it is in front of your right shoulder, lowering the point, and then executing thrust two. At the moment that the thrust reaches full extension, draw it back along the same path as you spring back into first position, raise the hand and bring the point up, and then perform parry two, as though parrying a thrust from your opponent.

Third thrust and parry:

Lower your sword hand to the level of your right hip and drop the point as you move forward into third position, turning your wrist so that the edge faces upward, and executing thrust three. At the moment that the thrust reaches full extension, spring back to first position, drawing the sword back along the same path; bring the point straight up, with the edge to the right and the hand at the level of the shoulder; and perform parry three, as though parrying a thrust from your opponent.

Moulinet:

Bring the point up and around, and execute a moulinet, sweeping the sword around you in a figure-eight motion, first to your right and then to your left. Return to second position and the engaging guard, and then return to first position and bring the sword up to a carry to finish the exercise.

This exercise is an essential step, and should be practiced relentlessly until it has been thoroughly mastered. First of all, just as with the manual, concentrate on committing the exercise to memory, step by step, being careful not to let any of the fine details slip. Check each element of footwork, attack, and defense against the descriptions and pictures given earlier in this book to be sure of your form. After you've mastered the form, begin working with breathing, directing the subtle energies of breath into each movement. Finally, work on speed and flow, until the entire exercise can be done in a single rush of precise movement. Once this stage has been reached, you're ready to proceed.

Practicing With A Partner

To go to the next step, you'll need a training partner who has reached at least the same stage of practice. This adds complexities of its own, although in nearly every case these can be overcome with a modest amount of patience and courtesy. It also marks the point at which live steel needs to be put aside, and safe practice weapons and protective gear put on.

If you don't yet have a training partner when you reach this stage, keep practicing the basic exercises, the manual, and the combined attack and defense exercise just given, while you look for a partner or wait for another student of the art to reach the necessary level of skill. There is literally no limit to the gains you can make by steady work with the fundamentals, and if a delay in moving on to partner practice means that you master the basics more thoroughly than you otherwise would have done, so much the better.

A few words about the proper attitude for partner training may not be out of place here. It's unfortunately common for people to approach training with others as a form of competition. Nothing could be more counterproductive. You and your partner will achieve the most if you are working together to learn, and to help each other learn—not to score points off each other, or to engage in a contest between overinflated egos.

You will get the best results, in other words, if you treat training sessions as an opportunity for mutual learning, not a contest. If you have been practicing longer or more regularly than your partner, or have natural advantages of quickness or dexterity, it's wise to temper your actions to your partner's abilities. If your partner is just beginning to learn how to use guards and parries effectively, for example, it's rarely a good idea to use maximum speed or tricky methods guaranteed to slip past his or her defenses. It's more productive to start with the basics, and let your partner build confidence and skill against these before going on to more elusive attacks.

Similarly, if you know (or think you know) more about swordsmanship than your partner, and notice something about his or her form that you think needs to be corrected, it's best to ask if your advice would be welcome before weighing in. If the answer is no, you may find it wise to keep your perceptions to yourself. To a refreshing extent, the Western martial arts have avoided the "master mystique" common to so many Asian systems; your superior skill or knowledge may make you a better swordsman or swordswoman than your partner, but it doesn't give you the right to tell other people what to do.

If you are practicing with someone who is better at swordplay than you are, in turn, it's often a good idea to listen to the advice he or she may offer, and to give his or her suggestions the benefit of the doubt. If you get discouraged by the difference between your abilities and your partner's—something that happens quite often, given our culture's obsession with competitive success—remember that you are both still learning, and that your own potential skill at swordplay is limited only by the time, effort, commitment and patience you are willing to devote to it.

Basic Partner Drill

The first step in training with a partner is a matter of learning to match attack and defense. This is done in the most basic possible way at first, and then made more complex step by step.

Start with both partners standing in first position, left arms tucked behind the back as before, right arms and swords fully extended toward each other. If you are using combat swords, the points of the swords should just touch; if you are using some other kind of practice sword with a full-length blade, the point of each sword should come to the guard of the other. This is the standard way of proving distance for partner drills, and the distance thus measured is the normal distance at which to begin swordplay.

Both partners then change to second position and take up the engaging guard. (Later, with practice, this and all other partner exercises can also be done from hanging guard, or with the participants in different guards; still, engaging guard is best to start with.) Combat swords will not quite reach each other at this range, while full-length blades should cross six or eight inches back from the point of each, with the blades turned edge to edge. The opponent's sword may be on either side of yours—on your left (which is called "inside guard") or your right ("outside guard"). Each of these positions has its own advantages and disadvantages, which you'll learn through experience.

Once both partners are settled in engaging guard, one partner, who will be called A, lunges forward into third position and attempts cut one against the other, who is B. B springs back into first position and responds with guard one, catching the foible of A's blade on the forte of his own. Both partners return to the engaging guard at second position. Then B lunges forward into first position and attempts cut one against A. A withdraws to first position and responds with guard one, catching the cut on the forte of his blade. They return to second position and the engaging guard again.

The same sequence is then done with cuts two through seven and guards two through seven. Each cut is made at third position and countered at first position; the partners return to second position and the engaging guard after each cut is made and countered. Next, the partners go through the thrusts and parries in the same way.

For this exercise, it's best to use parry one with thrust one, parry two with thrust two, and parry three with thrust three. Even though sword thrusts are usually stopped with one of the first four guards in actual combat, it's important to practice using the parries, so that you get some experience with them. The use of the parries against spear or bayonet thrusts is covered in Chapter Ten, where we'll deal with the use of the sword against the spear.

There are several important points to keep in mind while working with this exercise. First of all, it's best for the attacker to start off slowly at first, and to speed up the cuts and thrusts as the defending partner learns how to handle the clash of blades. The point of this exercise, it bears repeating, is not to score off your partner, but to enable both of you to make an effective transition from solo practice to the realities of combat. If you're going so fast that you can't maintain good form and integrate breath with your motions, you're going too fast for the time being. As the two of you become comfortable with increased speed, on the other hand, you should certainly accelerate the cuts until you are striking and responding at full combat speed.

Second, you should always remember to guard or parry an

actual attack with the forte of the blade, close to the hilt, where your strength is concentrated. The guard is always made with the edge, as noted above, while parries are made with the edge (in parries one and two) or the back of the sword (in parry three). Be careful not to let your form become sloppy, as bad habits learned at this stage can leave you vulnerable later on.

Third, the wide, sweeping cuts you use in the manual, while they're essential for teaching proper body dynamics, are out of place any time you're facing an opponent. Imagine a line connecting your solar plexus to that of your opponent. This is called the line of defense, and it plays a critical role in the tactics and strategy of swordsmanship.

In most situations, your sword hand should always stay as close as possible to the line of defense, moving above, below, or to the side to the minimum degree that your techniques actually require. When your hilt is on the line of defense, you can stop an attack from any direction before it lands. The further you stray from it, the more likely the opponent is to be able to hit you in whatever part of your body you leave uncovered. (This is why hanging guard is considered a somewhat risky posture; it sharply increases the possibilities for attack, but it moves the hilt well away from the line of defense.)

Finally, while it's important to keep the sword hand close to the line of defense, it's equally important not to let this habit produce weaknesses of its own. It can be tempting to use little, quick flicking cuts that come from the wrist and don't engage the rest of the body. This sort of cut is standard in modern sport saber fencing, since a sport fencer doesn't have to worry about his or her blows actually accomplishing anything! This temptation is one of the major factors that regular practice with the manual is meant to overcome, but it also needs to be watched here. Put yourself into the cuts, uniting the forward movement into third position with the dynamics of the cut and the subtle energy of breath, using your wrist as a fulcrum through which the movements of your body and arm are transformed into the swift whip-like arc of the blade.

Two-Step Drill

Once this simplest form of two-person sword drill has been practiced thoroughly, and both you and your partner are comfortable making and stopping attacks at full speed, you can go on to the next step, which is to add the transition between attack and defense. Begin as above, by both taking first position, proving distance, and moving into the engaging guard at second position. Then one of you—decide which one beforehand—says two numbers aloud, each between one and seven. (As an example, we'll use one and four.)

At this point, the other partner, whom we'll call A, lunges forward into third position and attempts the cut corresponding to the first number—cut one, in our example. The partner who chose the number, B, springs back to first position and uses guard one in response, and then immediately lunges forward to third position and attempts the cut corresponding to the second number—cut four, in our example. A, once his or her cut has been stopped, draws back to first position and counters B's cut with guard four. Both partners then return to engaging guard, and then the roles are reversed; A says two numbers between one and seven, B attacks immediately with the first cut named, and A responds with the appropriate guard and counters with the second cut. The partners then return to engaging guard, B names two more numbers, and the drill continues as above.

This drill is among the most important steps in making the transition to combat, since it includes a certain degree of unpredictability, and requires the students to move from attack to defense and back. After a few sessions, it will be clear that some combinations of cuts and guards are relatively easy to make, while others are a good deal less so. It's to your advantage to work with difficult as well as easy combinations, though. They may take more practice to do effectively, but once mastered they will allow you a greatly expanded range of options in combat.

Once the basic form outlined here has been practiced for some time, and you and your partner are both comfortable making and defending against attacks at full speed, add in the thrusts. For this purpose, treat thrust one as though it was "cut eight," thrust two as "cut nine," and thrust three as "cut ten." When partner A calls out "ten, two," in other words, partner B will respond with thrust three, which A will deflect with a parry or guard; A will then counter with cut two, which B will block with guard two.

An additional complexity can be added by specifying whether a thrust is to be met with a parry or a guard. When B says "six, parry nine," in other words, A will respond with cut six; once this is stopped with guard six, B will then attempt thrust two, which A must deflect with one of the three parries. If B says "six, guard nine," on the other hand, A must deflect B's thrust with a guard.

Three-Step Drill

This is exactly like the exercise just given, except that the partner who calls out numbers in each turn names three numbers rather than two, and all three techniques are then carried out. If A says "five, two, parry eight," in other words, B responds immediately by lunging forward and attempting cut five, which A blocks in first position with guard five. A then goes to third position and counters at once with cut two, which B stops with guard two. B responds with thrust one, which A must stop with a parry. Both partners then return to the engaging guard.

The full range of cuts, guards, thrusts and parries should be used in this exercise, and if both partners have studied and practiced them, the more advanced techniques covered later in this book can also be included. Once this exercise can be done with focus, grace, and economy of motion, with good form and proper breathing, at full speed, the partners are ready for free practice.

Chapter Eight
free practice

Free practice, or sparring, is the final element of training in swordsmanship, the closest equivalent to actual combat that can be done short of putting human lives on the line. Both partners begin in the same way as in the partner drills covered in Chapter Seven, taking first position, proving distance, and then entering into engaging or hanging guard. Each partner makes a single appel with his or her left foot on the floor, to signal that he or she is ready to begin. Once both have done so, either or both can make an attack, advance, retreat, traverse to either side, or carry out any other appropriate action. It's customary to stop when one of the partners has landed three solid cuts or thrusts on the other's body, or when either partner cries out "hold."

Many students want to move forward to free practice as soon as possible. If the foundation of skill has not been built by the preliminary exercises, the manual of the sword, and the attack and defense drills, though, free practice will quickly turn into random flailing about, of little use in teaching the handling of a real sword. Once you have worked the fundamental techniques of the art into your body, your subtle-energy body, and your awareness through systematic practice, on the other hand, free practice provides an arena in which those techniques can be mastered.

Several points will be found useful when taking up free practice. First of all, as mentioned above, the line of defense—the imaginary line connecting your solar plexus with that of your opponent—is the key to strategy in swordplay. Be aware of it constantly; keep your own hilt as close to it as you can, and try to lure your partner's hilt away from it if possible, striking at whatever part he or she uncovers.

Whenever you are not actually making an attack or defending against one, return to the engaging guard in second position. This is also the position you should adopt when advancing, retreating or traversing. It allows you to attack whenever an opening presents itself, and to defend yourself whenever your partner tries an attack. When you've gained some experience, hanging guard can also be used as a standard posture in free practice, and this is a very good way to get to know its strengths and weaknesses. In either guard, though, keep to second position when you're not actually attacking or defending. Staying in first or third position when it's not necessary is a common bad habit, and one that leads to needless vulnerability.

The proper use of the eyes is important. The sense of sight is easily misled in swordplay, and this is especially true if you look at your partner's weapon or sword hand. Instead, keep your gaze and your attention on the line of defense, striving to see the whole of your partner's body with a single glance. Try to sense your partner's movements by way of the *sentiment de fer*, the "sense of steel"; let your sword hand serve as your inner eyes. "You must think and see with the tips of your fingers" is a maxim quoted in the old books.

Strategy In Free Practice

There is a great deal of strategy in swordsmanship, and much of it has to do with putting together sequences of attacks that will mislead the opponent, or draw his or her sword out of the way for the fraction of a second needed to land an attack. It's often effective to follow up a high cut with a low one, or a low cut with a high one, forcing the opponent to cover the maximum distance with his blade in order to counter your attacks. A sequence of attacks, executed quickly, also has the advantage of taking the initiative away from the opponent, who will be so busy responding to your moves that he or she has no time to carry out an effective attack against you.

The entire body, it's worth noting, is a valid target in this system of swordsmanship; the sort of restricted target areas used in modern sport fencing, and in some historical reenactment systems, lead to a false idea of the use of the sword—and very often to bad habits of swordsmanship. Even apparently minor targets can be worth hitting in real combat, and so hits to them should be counted in free practice.

The foot, for example, may not seem like a very useful target. If you've ever stubbed your toes good and hard while barefoot, though, you know that pain in the foot can be a very potent distraction. In actual combat, if you can land a sold blow on the opponent's foot, the resulting pain and blood loss can leave him or her vulnerable to a lethal follow-up attack, and will at least hinder his or her mobility. (Such considerations may seem overly gruesome, but it always needs to be remembered that a sword is ultimately a tool for maiming and killing human beings—not a toy for playing games or a piece of equipment for sports.)

Different targets will be more or less vulnerable depending on the opponent's actions and habits. The head, the forward leg, and the sword arm are among the most common targets to keep in mind, but there are times when a straight thrust through the middle of the opponent's chest will work more effectively than any other technique. You should be careful not to let your attacks become predictable; if you always follow an attack to the head with one to the leg, your opponent will realize this and use it against you.

It's a commonplace in this tradition of swordsmanship that certain guards leave you in a better position to respond, while others leave you in a weaker one. The general rule is that guards one, five and seven, and the St. George guard, allow for the strongest responses. From these positions, all you have to do is extend the hand and turn the wrist to deliver a powerful cut very quickly. One standard and very effective technique is to stop the opponent's sword with one of these three guards, and then instantly, as soon as the blades come together, deliver a cut in response. Equally, it's a useful strategy to make a cut that forces the opponent into a weaker position before doing something that might otherwise leave you vulnerable.

One common failing is to hold a guard for too long. The moment the opponent's blade makes solid contact with yours, its momentum is spent, and it can't do significant damage until the opponent draws it back and attempts another cut. If you follow up with a cut or thrust immediately, your opponent will have to guard or parry at once if he or she plans on staying alive for more than a few seconds, and so won't have time to make that second cut.

If you have the opportunity to practice with a left-handed partner—whether or not you yourself are left-handed with a sword—you should certainly make use of it. The principles of swordsmanship don't change when facing a left-hander, but the differences are significant enough to give you trouble if you're not used to them. Remember that your opponent's strongest cuts and parries are on the side opposite the one you're used to, and trying to force him or her into what would be a weaker position for a right-hander can put you in plenty of trouble very quickly. Once again, practice is the key here. If you've followed the advice given earlier and practiced the manual and other exercises with both hands, a certain amount of additional work with your weak hand may make it possible for you to engage in free practice with either hand—and an ambidextrous swordsman or swordswoman is a tough opponent indeed.

Remember, finally, that the code of courtesy should govern your conduct at every moment when you are crossing swords with another person. Treat every interaction, whatever the limitations or conditions, as an opportunity to learn and to help someone else learn, and remember that as the first is a gift, the second is an honor.

Additional Techniques

The old handbooks of swordsmanship include several useful methods of attack and defense that aren't to be found in the standard manuals of the sword. All of these should be practiced on your own, and then put to use in free practice.

Defense against a leg cut:

When an opponent makes a cut or thrust toward your forward leg, you can block it with guards three or four, but there is another good way to handle this sort of attack. Simply spring back into first position, lean forward at the waist, and thrust straight at the attacker's face with the point of your sword. The attacker gets to choose between breaking off his attack in a hurry or running face first into your point.

Defense against a thrust:

In the same way, when an attacker makes a thrust or uses cut seven, stride left or right and cut at his or her arm. This technique is especially useful against the spear, but it also has its place when sword faces sword. It has to be practiced systematically until you can do it quickly and without hesitation; if the opponent realizes soon enough what you are doing, he or she can redirect the attack or volte to the other side and block your cut.

Feinting:

A feint is a false attack made to draw the opponent's blade in a given direction, opening the way to the real attack, which follows. There are an almost infinite number of possible feints, and the experienced swordsman will learn a good many of them. The two that were commonly taught, though, were the feint to the leg and the feint to the left side.

To practice the feint to the leg, start in outside guard, with your blade turned to the right and your opponent's sword to the right of yours. Raise your sword hand and press it to the right, bringing the forte of your blade against the foible of the opponent's, until the opponent's point is to the right of your body. Then drop your point in an arc as though striking at the outside of his or her forward leg. Without pausing, bring the sword up and around, lunge forward into third position, and make cut seven against the top of the opponent's head. Unless your opponent recognizes the first, downward movement as a feint, he or she will block downward as you cut from above.

To practice the feint to the left side, start in the same position and raise your hand as in the previous feint, and force the opponent's blade to the right, bringing your forte against the foible of the opposing blade. Then, with a quick movement of your wrist, bring your blade up and back so that it slips over the point of the opponent's sword, and feint cut one or cut five toward his or her left side. As he begins to respond, stop the cut, bring your sword over the opponent's head to his or her right side, and deliver cut two or cut six. Here again, unless the opponent recognizes that you are feinting, he or she will guard left as you cut right.

There are many other feints besides these, as mentioned above, but all of them work in essentially the same way. They may be worked out and tested in free practice, which will quickly show you which of them are effective and which are not.

There are a variety of ways to counter a feint. One of the best is to attack right through the middle of it—a technique known as a stop-hit. In the case of the feint to the leg, for example, as soon as your opponent begins the downward cut toward your leg, execute a thrust one at the middle of his or her chest. If your timing is right, your opponent will be unable to respond in time to stop the thrust. Even if he or she manages to do so, the attack will have to be abandoned.

Cut over the guard:

This technique is used to throw an opponent on the defensive. To practice it, start in engaging guard, swords crossed with the opponent. Move your sword hand forward until the forte of your blade is pressed against the foible of the opposing sword. Move your sword hand suddenly toward the opponent's blade, pushing it out of the way, and then raise your hand and cut downwards at the top of the opponent's wrist. If you draw back sharply with your blade across the wrist as you strike it, you can do enough damage to the wrist to make it difficult or impossible for the opponent to wield a sword at all. Even if this doesn't happen, the cut can disconcert an opponent and make it easier to follow up with something else.

There are two ways to counter this attack. First of all, you can be sure to keep a steady pressure against the opponent's blade, since it has to pull away from your blade before the attack begins. Second, you can disengage—that is, drop your point and then return to the engaging guard, catching the cut to your wrist on your blade and hilt.

Cut under the guard:

This is a tricky cut that can easily disarm or incapacitate an opponent. To practice it, start with the opposing sword to the right of your sword, in outside guard, and your edge turned to the right. Bring the forte of your blade against the foible of your opponent's, push it sharply to the right, and then suddenly bring your point back and around in a circle, as though you were doing a left moulinet. Going forward into third position, cut up against the underside of the opponent's sword arm, and spring back to second position and the engaging guard. Draw back sharply with the blade as you strike. If this attack succeeds, you will cut the tendons of the opponent's wrist and leave him or her defenseless.

There are, again, two ways to counter this. The first is simply to spring back to first position and make guard three, which will block the cut efficiently. The second—which is best done when the opponent has not pushed your sword quite far enough to the right—is to thrust straight ahead as the blade moves back and around, allowing the opponent to impale himself or herself on your sword as he or she lunges forward.

Chapter Nine
additional training methods

The exercises given already in this book provide the essential toolkit for learning swordsmanship. Several additional training methods, though, can usefully be added to this kit, as they build on the work already covered, and provide ways to develop further in your mastery of the craft of the sword. None of them, it should be said, can be found in the original collection of lore that forms the heart of this book. Still, all of them were used in nineteenth- and early twentieth-century physical culture and martial traditions in the West, and so are not out of place here.

Cutting And Thrusting Training

Perhaps the most important of these additional training methods is cutting and thrusting training. A sword, after all, is not just a steel club; it is intended to cut and stab the opponent, not merely bruise and batter him. Making it cut and thrust effectively takes a certain amount of practice, and no amount of swinging the sword through the air will do the trick. In order to learn to cut and thrust, in other words, you need to actually cut and thrust through physical objects.

The range of objects that can be used as targets for cutting and thrusting practice is limited only by your ingenuity and the requirements of safety and humanity. One of the best options is to use your sword to clear away brush and weeds that need to be removed. Practice until you can cut cleanly through each stalk or branch. A Christmas tree makes an equally useful target for the same type of work once the holidays are over. In both cases the results are also a good deal easier to fit into your compost bin, which can add a practical benefit to your training.

If you live in an apartment or your yard is impeccably kept, on the other hand, you'll need to look for something else. Cardboard tubes and boxes, rolled-up newspapers, pieces of styrofoam, plastic bottles full of water, and worn-out clothing filled with dry leaves or other padding materials can all be used. Again, concentrate on cutting and thrusting cleanly rather than just bashing in the sides of your targets. Any of these items can be hung on a rope, which will make them jump around as you hit at them and provide you with a more challenging target.

Precision Training

Several exercises are used to help the student develop the fine degree of precision needed to use the sword well in combat. All of these require a real sword with a sharp blade and point.

Candle exercise:

One of the classic methods of precision training is the famous candle exercise. Light a candle—a tall taper in a relatively low, flat stand works well for this—and set it on a piece of furniture that can be scratched or cut with impunity. (It's often a good idea to build a stand out of lumber, so you don't have to worry about the results if you miss the candle and hit the stand.) The flame of the candle can be anywhere from three to six feet above the ground, and there should be room to swing a sword freely to both sides.

Stand in front of the candle, in either engaging guard or hanging guard, and then make either cut five or cut six at the flame. The goal is to put out the flame with a single cut without touching the candle. Focus, accuracy and speed are all required to accomplish this.

A more advanced version of the same exercise involves setting up a series of candles at different heights around your practice space. Stand in the center with your sword in the scabbard and your hands at your sides. At a given signal—whihc can come from a training partner, or from an alarm clock you've set to go off in a minute or two and put behind you where you can't see it—draw the sword and start putting out candles with a succession of cuts, as quickly as you can. Your goal is to put out all the flames without wasting a cut, hitting a candle, or using any more time than you absolutely have to. This exercise is a good way to help develop the reflexes you'll need in the constantly changing realm of actual combat.

Paper exercise:

For this exercise, you'll need to hang a sheet of paper by a piece of string from the ceiling, if your practice space is indoors, or a convenient tree branch if it's outdoors. Draw your sword, and begin cutting and thrusting at the paper. The goal here is to actually cut and pierce the paper, not simply bat it around or tear it; this requires a sharp blade and solid, well-focused attacks.

Start out with a relatively heavy, easy-to-cut paper like construction paper; when this is easy to cut and pierce, change to something lighter. When you can cut a piece of light rice paper cleanly in half with a single blow, you'll be well on your way to mastery.

For an additional challenge, do this outdoors on a windy day. Trying to cut the paper as it dances around freely at the end of the string is a serious challenge, and if you can meet it successfully there will be very little in the realm of swordsmanship that you can't handle.

Fruit exercise:

For this exercise, you'll need a post on which a piece of fruit, or some other small soft object, can be placed. The top of the post should be about the level of your heart. Put the fruit in place, and then thrust or cut at it. The goal here is to impale it on the point of your sword, if you're thrusting, or to cut it in half, if you're cutting. If your sword isn't very sharp, and the thrust or cut isn't made with a high degree of focus and precision, you'll simply knock the fruit off the post.

Impact Training

There is a world of difference between the way that a sword handles when it's swung through empty air and the way it responds when it hits an opponent's weapon—or, for that matter, an opponent. It takes practice to learn to control a sword in the aftermath of an attack, whether or not the attack penetrates the opponent's defenses.

Tire exercise:

Probably the best option for a modern student of swordsmanship is to hang a used tire by a rope from a sturdy tree branch, just as if you were making a swing. The center of the tire should be about the level of your heart. This becomes your target for the full range of cuts and thrusts.

You can use your real sword on the hanging tire, as long as the tire doesn't have metal belts or studs anywhere in it, but it's just as effective to get a piece of 1" hardwood dowel the same length as your sword. The advantage of a hardwood sword is that the tire will last much longer, and can be used as a swing by your kids when you're not pounding the bejesus out of it. Whatever you use, though, plan on wearing a glove and face protection; scraps of tire will go flying in all directions if you're using live steel, while a wooden sword can break unexpectedly and send splinters and scraps of itself back at you.

Grip And Wrist Training

One set of muscles that are usually underdeveloped in modern people, and thus need to be strengthened and developed to meet the demands of swordsmanship, are the muscles of the hand and wrist. Although effective movements of the sword unfold from the body core and are shaped by the positions and motions of the whole body, the wrist and hand form the fulcrum through which these flow into the sword. If that fulcrum is weak, your cuts and thrusts will be inaccurate and inefficient. The following exercises will help you to avoid this. They should be done on both sides for maximum benefit.

Broom exercise:

Start with an ordinary household broom. Take hold of the end of the handle, using the standard sword grip, with the thumb on top. Place your elbow against your side and hold your forearm out level, with the head of the broom resting on the floor in front of you. Now, slowly raise the broom head until the handle is slanting upwards at a 45° angle. Lower it again until the head just touches the floor, and then raise it again. Raise and lower the head a total of ten times, if you can; it's harder than it sounds. Don't let the weight of the broom come to rest on the floor, and don't let the handle go up past a 45ø angle; either one of these mistakes will give the muscles of your hand and wrist a rest, and cheat you of some of this exercise's benefits.

Next, turn your hand over so that the thumb is underneath, as though you were doing thrust three. Repeat the exercise, raising and lowering the broom slowly as before. This works a different set of muscles in the hands and wrists, and helps build all-round strength in the muscles and ligaments.

Heavy sword exercise:

For this exercise, you'll need a sword or a sword-substitute that weighs at least twice what your real sword does. One good option here is to buy one of the decorative swords sold in some import shops, with a heavy pot- metal blade; these are useless for most purposes but fine for heavy sword practice. Lacking this, get a piece of iron plumbing pipe the same length as your sword.

To use the heavy sword, simply go through the manual of the sword several times, slowly, paying attention to form and breath. Keep your movements as smooth and steady as you can. This is a very effective way to build strength throughout your arms and shoulders, and the weight and drag of the heavy sword will also force you to learn the most efficient ways to move the blade. One session of heavy sword training a week is usually enough, if you keep it up until your arms are good and tired.

Visualization Training

A less muscular but equally valuable addition to your training schedule is visualization training, in which you carry out the manual of the sword and other training exercises with your mind rather than your body. While it's not a substitute for physical practice, it has some important benefits to offer. It helps develop mental clarity and a thorough grasp of technique, and it trains the nervous system in coordinating patterns of movement. Sports researchers have also found that the nerve responses set off by visualization training actually improve muscular tone, and produce measurable benefits in terms of strength, speed and stamina. To imagine using a muscle, it turns out, is to stimulate the connections between muscle and nerve and to bring extra oxygen and nutrition to the tissue.

Chapter 9 – Additional Training Methods

To do visualization training, start out with the first breathing exercise from Chapter Four; sit in the position described there, and do several cycles of the Complete Breath. Then, with eyes closed or open—however you find it easiest to build up imaginary pictures in your mind—imagine yourself standing in the middle of an imaginary practice space, with your sword in your hand.

Make the imagery as clear and precise as possible. Don't simply use visual imagination; feel the hilt of the sword in your grip, the placing of your limbs and torso in first position, the floor or ground beneath your feet. As far as possible, try to indwell the image—that is, don't watch the image of yourself from outside, like a spectator, but imagine it as though you were there, in the imagined body about to begin your sword practice.

Feel the movements of your body and the shifting weight of the sword as you carry out the exercises. You'll probably need to do them very slowly at first, just as though you're learning how to do them for the first time with your physical body. This is fine; concentrate on form, and try to make your imagined movements clean and exact. Carry out whatever exercise you have in mind, then imagine yourself returning to your original position in the middle of the imaginary practice space. Return your attention to your physical body, do several cycles of the Complete Breath, and then stretch, stand up, move around and turn your attention to the physical world. If you feel vague or disconnected, eat something—few things will bring you back to the physical level faster than a full stomach—or engage in some fairly strenuous physical activity.

The manual of the sword is your first task in visualization practice. You should work with it exclusively until you can do it in your imagination, with form, breath, and speed, at least as well as you can do it physically. Once you've achieved this, go on to the exercises in Chapter Seven, taking them one at a time and practicing them thoroughly in your imagination. Start with the solo exercise, and go on to the partner exercises only if you also have a physical partner to train with.

The visualized partner practices should be done with an

imaginary partner, whom you can build up in as much detail as you like. (Don't be surprised if your imaginary partner develops a personality and a mind of his or her own, like the people who appear in your dreams.) Finally, go to work on free practice with your imaginary partner, incorporating spear training methods from Chapter Ten if you wish.

Blindfold Training

While the eyes and the ordinary senses are important in swordsmanship, much of the perceptiveness that makes for mastery of the sword comes through more intuitive channels. These subtler ways of sensing can evolve into a seemingly supernatural ability to anticipate and forestall an opponent's actions.

In reality, of course, nothing supernatural is involved. The perceptive swordsman or swordswoman simply develops natural capacities that most of us leave neglected. These capacities are a function of the higher mental and spiritual powers that are present in each human being, hidden away behind a veil formed by our obsession with the material.

There are a wide range of exercises that can be used to develop the higher powers, but few of them can be used effectively with a wide range of spiritual paths, and even fewer have any direct application to swordsmanship. One that meets both these criteria is blindfold training. In order to do it, you'll need a partner, practice swords, and a good blindfold—one that closes off your entire field of vision. Patience, persistence, and the ability to deal with frustration are also necessities, since it may well take several years of regular practice before you start getting reliable results.

Preliminary exercise:

The first step in blindfold training can be taken without a partner or swords—although having someone to help put the blindfold on you is probably a good idea, unless you're unusually dextrous. Simply put on the blindfold and stand still. Without physically moving or reaching out, try to feel the space around you. Avoid building up mental imagery, trying to imagine where this or that thing might be; simply feel the subtle qualities and character of the space around you.

This should be done several times at least before you do any other phase of blindfold training. If you can arrange it, it's particularly valuable to spend time blindfolded in different places. Half an hour spent blindfolded outdoors in a natural environment can make for an extraordinary experience, although in this case you should be sure to have someone watching nearby. Once you're used to feeling the space around you, you can go on to the blindfold exercises themselves.

First blindfold exercise:

To start with, one of the partners, A, is blindfolded, and stands in first position, without a sword. The other, B, takes a practice sword, stands at a convenient distance, and very slowly makes cut one or two toward A's right or left shoulder. A tries to perceive the cut before it lands, and gestures with his or her empty sword hand toward the side from which the cut seems to be coming. B finishes the cut by tapping the blade against A's shoulder, then draws the sword back, pauses, and makes another cut, either one or two. B should be careful not to simply alternate one-two-one-two, but should avoid any predictable pattern, making two or three of one cut in a row at times, and pausing for intervals of random length between cuts. Twenty cuts is a good maximum for each practice session; after that, the partners change roles, and B is blindfolded while A makes cuts.

At this stage of the practice, only cuts one and two should be used. The cuts should be made in extreme slow motion, and B should concentrate on the cut as it's made, putting intention and breath into it, to maximize A's chances of sensing it. Both partners should be silent, and other sources of distraction should be kept at a minimum.

Once the direction of the approaching cut can be reliably sensed eight or nine times out of ten, you're ready to go on to the next step.

Second blindfold exercise:

This exercise is exactly like the last one, except that the blindfolded partner has a sword, and both partners wear full protective gear. B makes cuts one and two to A's right and left shoulders, exactly as in the first blindfold exercise. Now, however, A responds by moving his or her sword to block the cuts, using guards one and two. As before, B should make the cuts very slowly at first, concentrating on each cut and breathing into it, and should be careful to avoid any predictable pattern in the order or timing of cuts. Silence and the avoidance of distractions are as important here as in the first exercise; so is a relaxed atmosphere, and so is patience. After the blindfolded partner has learned to respond correctly to unseen cuts in slow motion, the speed of the cuts can be increased gradually.

Once this exercise has been practiced for a while, and the student has begun to achieve a certain degree of skill, it becomes an important source of lessons in the reality of the subtle senses. There are few things in the world that are more convincing than the sound of clashing steel as you parry a cut you can't see! This is of real importance, for confidence has a powerful influence on the ability to access these half-hidden perceptions. To a great extent, you can use this ability to the extent that you believe you can.

Third blindfold exercise:

This exercise begins exactly like the last one, but in this case all seven cuts are used, and A must counter them with all seven guards. Again, B should start out with very slow cuts, and not speed up until A can successfully counter eight or nine cuts out of ten. Later, when the whole range of cuts can be done at speed,

Chapter 9 – Additional Training Methods

the thrusts can be incorporated as well. The whole process may take a good deal of time and patience, since the additional cuts can be confusing to the inner senses at first. Perseverance and regular practice are the keys, here as elsewhere.

As you work with the entire sequence of blindfold exercises, it's important to try to integrate the skills you're learning with the rest of your training in swordsmanship. In other types of practice, try to sense as well as see your partner's actions; when doing blindfold training, be sure to pay attention to proper form and breath, so that the movements inspired by your intuitive perceptions are vigorous, effective and precise, not random flailings in the air.

Chapter Ten
sword and spear

The history of Western swordsmanship, as chronicled in Chapter One, has left many traces in the system of swordplay taught in this book, and one of them will be central to this final chapter. Throughout the seventeenth, eighteenth, and nineteenth centuries, as we've seen, the sword was the weapon of officers and gentlemen. In warfare on land, it was carried and used by cavalry—which remained an aristocrat's branch of service up until the early 20th century—and by the officers and NCOs in charge of infantry and artillery units.

The vast majority of soldiers, on the other hand, carried different weapons. In the seventeenth century, they carried pikes and matchlock muskets. Starting in the eighteenth century—

when the invention of the bayonet allowed pike and musket to be combined into a single weapon—muskets equipped with bayonets were the common soldier's fighting arm. Certain types of spear, such as the spontoon, also remained in use in some armies into the early years of the nineteenth century. Things were much the same on the oceans; although cutlasses and other naval swords were a good deal more common than on land, short heavy spears called boarding pikes were a common weapon, and all hands from the captain to the scullery boys were expected to defend the ship when an enemy vessel came alongside and boarding parties surged over the gunwales.

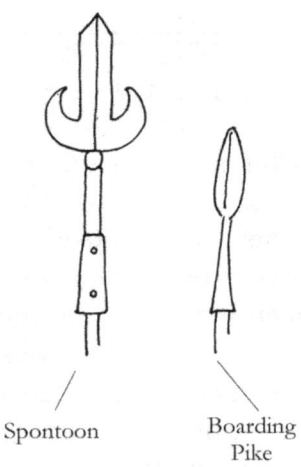

Spontoon   Boarding Pike

Diagram 10-1

A swordsman thus had to be ready to deal with spear and bayonet thrusts, not merely with other swords, whenever the tide of battle brought him into hand-to-hand combat. The resulting techniques and training methods make up a significant part of the eighteenth- and nineteenth-century sword traditions that gave rise to the system taught here. I've included them partly for the sake of completeness, and partly because the addition of spear techniques provides an interesting and useful set of variations from the ordinary routine of sword training.

Spear Fundamentals

For the purposes of this chapter, we'll assume that the weapon being used is a standard spear, rather than a bayonet or a polearm of some other kind. (The techniques for all polearms, including the bayonet, are essentially the same, but the spear is simpler and also somewhat easier to use.) The parts of a spear are shown in diagram 10-2.

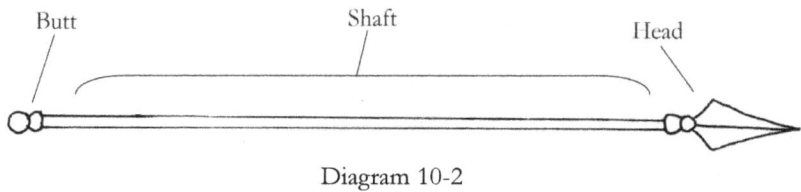

Diagram 10-2

The head is the business end, provided with a sharpened steel blade that, in most cases, can cut as well as thrust. The shaft is usually of wood, and fits into a socket in the head; metal bars called langets sometimes extend from the head along the upper part of the shaft, to keep the head from being cut off by a solid sword cut. The butt, on the other end, was usually tipped with a butt cap of steel. This helped to balance the weight of the head, and also allowed the spearman or spearwoman to use both ends of the spear as offensive weapons.

Just as it's necessary to have a real sword in order to learn and practice swordsmanship, there's not much point in trying to learn the use of the spear if you don't have one. Like modern swords, spears available nowadays run all the way from excellent weapons to useless junk. Points you should look for include:

1. The shaft should be between five and eight feet long, and made of hardwood, not the sort of softwood doweling most lumber stores sell. It should be straight and without knots. It should be smooth and treated with a good finish; if the manufacturer didn't do this, plan on sanding it down with fine grit sandpaper until it feels as smooth as glass to your hand,

and then oiling it with linseed oil. The shaft is the most important part of a spear; a good shaft can make up for a mediocre head, but the best head in the world is worth little on a warped or brittle shaft.

2. The head should be of steel, not cast iron or some pot metal alloy, and it should have been forged, not merely cast or machined into shape. Many of the same tips discussed in Chapter Two for examining a sword can be put to use here as well. The head should be sturdy, free from useless decoration, and able to take a fine edge.

3. The butt cap can be of any sturdy metal, but a relatively soft steel is best.

The proper grip for the spear comes naturally to most people. Grasp the shaft with the left hand, thumb toward the head, about halfway along the shaft's length. Grasp the shaft with the right hand, thumb toward the head, between six inches and a foot from the butt cap, depending on the length of the spear. While there were variations, and some methods of spear combat taught the student to switch grips in certain situations, this basic grip was standard in most systems and will serve for all the techniques taught here.

The stances for the spear also come easily, but if you've practiced the footwork for the sword as given in Chapter Five on one side only, you have some relearning to do. With a sword, of course, the strong hand—the right hand, for most people—is usually forward. When using a spear or any other polearm, by contrast, the strong hand is held back, allowing it to put maximum force into thrusts. If you're right-handed, then, your right foot is forward when you're using a sword, but your left foot is forward when you're using a spear.

This aside, sword and spear footwork are all but identical. First, second and third position are done exactly the same for the two weapons, except that the feet are reversed, and the same is true of the advance, retreat, traverse, step, pass, stride and volte.

If you didn't learn the footwork on both sides, it's a good idea to go through all the footwork exercises in Chapter Five again with your feet positioned for spear work, to make sure that your hips, legs and feet will do what you want them to do in combat. Other sword exercises, such as the fourth breathing exercise from Chapter Four, are also very much worth integrating into spear training.

The Manual Of The Spear

The manual of the spear is somewhat simpler than that of the sword, since there are fewer techniques in the basic spear repertoire. With one exception, though, the same basic principles apply. The exception is a matter of stance; since the spear is a good deal longer and heavier than the sword, most of the manual is done in second position, rather than first.

Starting position and carry:

Begin in first position, left foot pointed forward, right foot behind it and pointing toward the right. The spear is positioned vertically, resting against your right shoulder; the shaft is held by your right hand about six inches from the butt cap. The head of the spear is well above your head, and your left hand is at your side. Your right hand grasps the shaft with the thumb and forefinger, with the other fingers behind the shaft, much as in the carry for the sword. This position is the carry for the spear.

Chapter 10 – Sword and Spear

Diagram 10-3

Now step forward with your left foot, taking second position. At the same moment, raise your left arm out in front of you, opening your left hand with the palm up, and draw your right hand back slightly, straightening your fingers so that you cna take a firm grip. Allow the spear to fall forward, and catch it with your left hand. Grip the spear firmly with both hands; your right hand should be at your right hip, and your left hand is raised, so that the point of the spear comes in front of your left shoulder. This is the engaging guard for the spear.

Diagram 10-4

Prove distance:

Now extend your left arm forward to its furthest reach, and shift your weight forward. Loosen your left hand's grip on the shaft slightly, and push the right hand forward, allowing the shaft to slide through the left hand until the left hand comes close to the right one, extending the spear to its maximum reach in front. Sweep the point of the spear out to each side, to about a 45 degree angle. This makes sure that there's nothing within striking range ahead of you. Now draw back the right hand, allowing the shaft to slide through the left hand until the hands are at their usual position. Step back to first position, and bring the point of the spear up and overhead in an arc, by bringing your right hand up in front of you and your left hand to rest on top of your right shoulder. Make sure the spear doesn't hit anything above or behind you. (The manual of the spear doesn't involve significant movements to the side, so it's not necessary to prove distance in that direction.) Return to second position and resume the engaging guard. At this point, you're ready to begin the techniques of the manual.

Circle right and left:

Make a circle with the point, about a foot in diameter, going up, to the right, down, and back to where you started. Then make another circle, up, to the left, down, and back. These simple moves are actually the foundation for some of the spear's most effective techniques. Feinting on one side of an opponent's sword, circling around to the other, and thrusting is a mainstay of spear tactics.

High thrust:

Thrust the point of the spear straight forward at the face of an imaginary opponent in front of you, straightening your left arm to its full extension, and bringing the right arm forward, in front of your right hip. The butt of the spear should be at the level of the hip, outside the right forearm. The spear slants up at a diagonal. As soon as the thrust is delivered, return to the engaging guard.

Diagram 10-5

Low thrust:

Thrust the point of the spear forward and down, toward the belly of an imaginary opponent in front of you, straightening your left arm to its furthest extension, and raising the right arm above the level of your right shoulder. The butt of the spear should be at the level of your chin, outside the right forearm, where it protects the face and neck. The spear slants down at a diagonal. As soon as the thrust is delivered, return to the engaging guard.

Diagram 10-6

Long thrust:

Thrust the point of the spear straight ahead by loosening the grip of your left hand on the shaft and pushing the right hand forward forcefully, until the two hands come within six inches or so of each other, and the spear slides out to its full extension. As soon as the thrust is delivered, pull the right hand back to the right hip, letting the shaft slide back through the left hand until you have returned to the ordinary grip, and resume the engaging guard.

Diagram 10-7

Vertical butt strike:

Push the right hand forward and up, and bring the left hand back in an arc to rest atop your right shoulder, bringing the butt of the spear up in an arc to strike the groin, solar plexus or chin of an imaginary opponent. The spear shaft should be horizontal, with the head pointing straight behind you, as the movement finishes.

Diagram 10-8

Vertical cut:

From the end position of the vertical butt strike, push the left hand forward and pull the right back to the right hip, cutting down in an arc with the head of the spear. The movement finishes in the engaging guard.

Diagonal butt strike:

Push the right hand forward, as in the vertical butt strike, but this time bring the left hand back to the left shoulder so that the butt of the spear rises along a diagonal arc, striking the groin, solar plexus or chin of an imaginary opponent. The movement finishes with the shaft horizontal and the head pointing back behind you. At this point, jab straight forward with the butt of the spear, and then draw the butt back to where it was before the jab.

Diagram 10-9

Diagonal cut:

From the endpoint of the diagonal butt strike, push the left hand forward and draw the right hand back to your hip, bringing the head of the spear cutting down and across in a diagonal arc. The movement finishes in the engaging guard.

Diagram 10-10

Right parry:

From the engaging guard, drop the right hand down, and push the left hand sharply to the right, so that the spear is to the right of your body. Return to the engaging guard as soon as the parry is complete.

Diagram 10-11

Left parry:

From the engaging guard, drop the right hand down and then move right and left hands both to the left, turning to the left at the waist if necessary, so that the spear is to the left of your body. Return to the engaging guard as soon as the parry is complete.

Diagram 10-12

Right low parry:

From the engaging guard, raise the right hand up to the height of your head and push the left hand to your right, so that the spear is to the right of your body, with the point angling downwards. Return to the engaging guard as soon as the parry is complete.

Diagram 10-13

Left low parry:

From the engaging guard, raise the right hand up to the level of your head and then carry it across to the left, with your elbow raised so that you look out from under your arm. Meanwhile move the left hand to your left, so that the spear is to the left of your body, with the point angling downwards. Return to the engaging guard as soon as the parry is complete.

Diagram 10-14

High parry:

From the engaging guard, raise both hands sharply upwards until the shaft of the spear is above and in front of the head, the point angled forward and to your left, the head and butt of the spear at the same level. Return to the engaging guard as soon as the parry is complete.

Diagram 10-15

This completes the manual of the spear; from the final engaging guard, return to first position and the carry. As with the manual of the sword, the manual of the spear needs to be practiced relentlessly before you go on to the rest of the spear technique given here. As with the sword manual, too, form, breath, and speed should be your three targets, mastering each one before you go onto the next.

Attack and Defense

Once the manual has been learned thoroughly, the next step—just as with the sword—consists of integrating attack, defense, and footwork. The following drill will be helpful in this connection.

Start in first position with the spear at the carry, then prove distance and take up the engaging guard, just as in the manual of the spear.

First division:

Make a low thrust to the belly of an imaginary opponent, moving from second to third position. Spring back to second position, making a right parry, and instantly move forward into third position, making a vertical butt strike and following it with a vertical cut. Return to second position and the engaging guard.

Second division:

Make a low thrust to the belly of an imaginary opponent, moving from second to third position. Spring back to second position, make a left parry, and instantly lunge forward into third position, making a diagonal butt strike, jabbing with the butt, and following up with a diagonal cut. Return to second position and the engaging guard.

Third division:

Make a high thrust to the face of an imaginary opponent, moving from second to third position. Spring back to second position, make a right low parry, and instantly move forward into third position and deliver a low thrust to the belly. Return to second position and engaging guard.

Fourth division:

Make a high thrust to the face of an imaginary opponent, moving from second to third position. Spring back to second position, making a left low parry. Instantly lunge into third position, bring the right hand diagonally down across your body to your right hip and push your left hand forward, executing a diagonal cut. Follow up with a low thrust to the belly. Return to second position and engaging guard.

Fifth division:

Make a low thrust to the belly of an imaginary opponent, moving from second to third position. Spring back to second position, making a high parry. Instantly stride either left or right, lower your hands, and make a long thrust at an angle to the imaginary opponent's belly, shooting the spear out through the left hand. Draw the spear back, take the usual grip again, and return to your original position, resuming the engaging guard. Finish by returning to first position with the spear at the carry.

This drill should be practiced in the same way as the sword drills, concentrating on form, breath, and speed respectively, until you can do the whole thing in a precise, focused and effective manner at full combat speed. Once this has been achieved, create sequences of your own—combining attacks, defenses, and footwork in the same way—and practice them until you can do them with the same degree of skill. Any of the additional training exercises in Chapter Nine may also be put to use in spear training, to develop your abilities with the spear and present your sword-carrying opponent with a more serious challenge.

Partner Exercises:

The next step in training involves pitting the sword against the spear in a set of systematic two-person exercises, like the ones used to teach sword combat. For this phase of practice, you'll need a training spear, which is simply a six- to eight- foot length of 7/8" or 1" diameter dowel, tipped with a heavily padded head and butt. The padding is the same at both ends: an inch thick layer of dense foam rubber wrapped around the shaft of the spear, with at least another inch thick layer of soft foam rubber over it, and the whole pad securely fastened with duct tape. The foam must extend at least a foot behind each end of the shaft, and must project at least four inches out past the dowel, with the hollow space between the end of the dowel and the tip of the spear filled with more soft foam. Each business end should be covered by a flat disk of soft foam rubber to help spread out the impact. The whole should look like diagram 10-16.

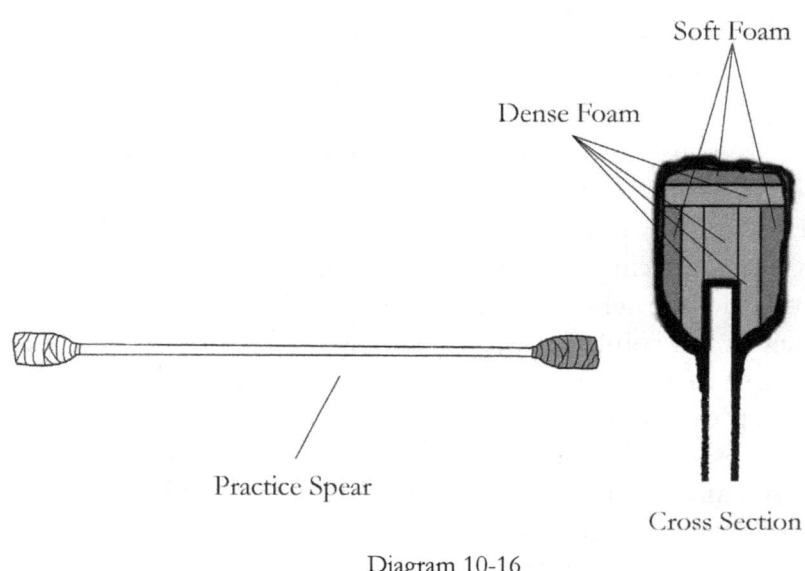

Diagram 10-16

One end of the practice spear should be marked with colored tape; this end will represent the head. The other represents the butt. Both ends, of course, will be used in training and combat, but it's a good idea to keep the difference between them in mind. On a real spear, the head is a good deal more effective than the butt, and should be used by preference in attacks meant to end a fight once and for all.

The protective gear used in spear training is essentially the same as that for sword training, with one addition. If at all possible, the partner using the spear should wear heavy padded gloves. Boxing gloves, kempo gloves, or hockey gloves are the sort of protection needed here. The spear does not protect the hand the way the hilt of a sword does, and one of the most important tactics a swordsman or swordswoman uses against the spear is a cut to the hand. Using robust hand protection makes it possible for this to be practice without risking pain, bruising, or damage to the small bones of the hand.

The following exercises all assume that you and your partner have both worked your way through the whole course of training given already in this book, and have enough experience with the methods already covered to work through partner drills with the spear quickly and efficiently. The spear is a weapon in its own right, of course, and not just a help to sword training, but its place in this book is more or less limited to the latter. (It's for this reason that I have not included material on using the spear against another spear, or any other sort of weaponry besides the sword.)

Parrying The Spear

As mentioned earlier, the three parries are the primary methods used by a swordsman or swordswoman to block thrusts with a spear, bayonet, boarding pike, or any similar weapon. For sword thrusts, the first four guards are quicker, and speed rather than force is more crucial in deflecting a sword. Spears and other weapons of the same type are slower but require more force to be turned aside. The following drills will help begin teaching the particular skills involved.

First parrying exercise:

For the first stage, one partner, A, takes the practice spear, and puts on protective gloves. The other partner, B, puts on full protective gear and takes a practice sword. To prove distance, B extends his or her sword straight out toward A from first position. A then extends the spear as far as possible to the front, without allowing the shaft to slide through the left hand. The point of the spear should come to the hilt of B's sword.

B then bends his sword arm, brings the hilt down and raises the point, as though entering into engaging guard, but stays in first position. A enters engaging guard and makes a high thrust toward B's right shoulder, moving forward into third position. B parries it with parry one and brings the parry all the way around, cutting at A's forward hand from below, as A recovers to engaging guard. A then makes a high thrust toward B's left shoulder, and B parries it with parry two, again letting the parry continue around to cut at A's hand from below. A makes a low thrust toward B's belly, and B parries it with parry three, then brings the sword up and around by turning his or her wrist and cuts at A's forward hand from above.

A continues with a thrust to B's right shoulder, which B parries as before. The exercise continues in the same way, with A thrusting to right shoulder, left shoulder, and belly, and B responding with parries one, two and three. Once B has had enough of parrying, the partners switch roles.

Second parrying exercise:

The preliminaries for this second stage of training are identical to those for the first stage. After proving distance, B drops into engaging guard, and makes a single appel on the floor with his forward foot, signaling that he or she is ready. A then starts making thrusts at B with the spear, aiming them high, low, to one side and to the other. B parries each of them using the first, second or third parries, or a right or left moulinet. In every case, the parry should be continued into a cut against A's hand. After B has had enough, the partners switch roles, and B wields the spear while A parries it with the sword.

For the first few practice sessions, A's thrusts should start off slowly, to give B a chance to learn the mechanics of the parries and moulinets, and work on the essential factors of form, breath, and speed. Thereafter, as B develops skill, the thrusts can come more quickly, until A is thrusting at full speed, varying direction and timing at will.

The final stage in this exercise is the integration of butt strikes and spear cuts. These are countered with the guards rather than the parries. Guards must be made much more forcefully against these techniques than against sword cuts, since the spear has a great deal more momentum behind it and will be much harder to stop effectively. Once again, these should be started slowly at first, and A should increase the speed and power of these attacks only as B develops his or her skill in responding to them.

Parrying The Sword

Just as the sword must parry the spear, of course, the spear must parry the sword. Again, basic drills of the sort already given are the best way to start developing the skills involved.

Third parrying exercise:

For this exercise, the partner with the practice spear, A, puts on protective gear. B takes a practice sword. The two partners prove distance, just as in the first parrying exercise, and A takes up the engaging guard.

B then makes cut one toward A's left shoulder. A counters it with a left parry. B makes cut two toward A's right shoulder, which A counters with a right parry. B makes cut three, which A counters with a left low parry; B follows with cut four, which A counters with a right low parry. B then makes cut seven, which A counters with a high parry. The process then repeats exactly as before, with B making cuts one, two, three, four, and seven in that order, and A parrying accordingly. Once A has had enough of parrying, the partners switch roles.

Fourth parrying exercise:

Like the second parrying exercise, this one opens up the field to the entire range of sword attacks, which the partner using the spear must parry effectively. The preliminaries are the same as those for the third parrying exercise. This time, the partner with the sword, B, cuts at A with any of the seven cuts, and A parries them with the spear. As before, B starts off with relatively slow cuts, increasing speed as A becomes more familar with the parrying capacities of the spear.

Once A can handle any of the cuts, B adds the three thrusts to his or her repertoire, and when A has learned to counter these effectively, B can make use of any of the additional methods, including feints and cuts over and under the guard. All these are introduced at slow speed, and then brought up to full speed and power as A's learning curve permits.

The four parrying exercises should be practiced until both partners can safely and efficiently handle any sword attack with a spear, and any spear attack with a sword. Once this level has been achieved, the final step is free practice between sword and spear.

Free Practice: Sword Versus Spear

Free practice with mixed weapons is carried out in much the same way as free practice with swords. The major difference lies in the strategies involved, and much of that needs to be learned through actual experience. A few comments may be useful to provide some initial guidance, but the real learning begins once you and your partner are facing each other in the midst of the practice space. According to the old manuals, the sword was considered to be the more effective weapon of the two, but it's always worth remembering that it's not weapons but the people wielding them that make the difference in combat. A spear in the hands of a competent wielder is far from negligible, and a swordsman or swordswoman who deals with one incautiously is likely to end up understanding what shishkebab meat feels like.

In facing an opponent armed with any weapon of the spear type, a swordsman or swordswoman has two important advantages. The first is that the sword is a good deal quicker and easier to maneuver than the spear. The second is that the sword protects the hand, while the spear does not. These two advantages must be combined with good technique and effective strategy to overcome the spear's advantages of reach and momentum.

Your first goal, when faced with a spear, is to get close enough to carry out an effective attack. Advance in engaging guard, closing the distance between you and your opponent, and raising or lowering your hand to match any upward or downward movement of the spear. If the opponent thrusts, parry, spring forward into third position and cut at his or her hands, arms or face, using the momentum of the parry to add speed to the counterattack. If the opponent stays on the defensive, feint and attack any convenient target. A cut over or under the guard against his or her forward arm is often worth trying, if you can be sure the spear point won't hit you in the middle of your attack.

Be aware at all times of the possibility of a butt strike. This can be countered easily if you are watching for it, but if it takes you by surprise it can put you out of combat in short order. Your most effective move when an opponent attempts a butt strike against you is to respond with the appropriate guard in such a way that your sword meets the opponent's hand, rather than the shaft of the spear.

The long thrust by the spear is also something to watch out for, since it can strike you when you may think you're well out of range. Keep your guard up no matter how far away your opponent is. If you can trick your partner into making a long thrust when you're ready for it, you can easily knock the spear aside, close in suddenly and deliver an attack before he or she has a chance to respond.

In some cases, especially when the strike is delivered with great force, it can be a good idea to volte or stride to one side or the other while guarding. This gets your body out of the way of the strike, and can put you in a position where you can deliver a counterattack before your opponent has any hope of recovering.

Another technique good for forceful strikes, if you use a single-edged sword, is a reinforced guard—that is, a guard backed up by your other hand. This is done simply by supporting the back of the blade, a foot or so back from the tip, with the palm of the hand that's not holding the hilt. It's rarely possible to do this effectively when your hand starts out behind your back, in the usual practice position, so you may find it useful to practice now and then with your hand out in front. This is also a necessity if you want to try to grab the shaft of the spear—a very effective technique in some situations, since it can paralyze the spearman's ability to respond for the second or so you need to close in and strike.

If you are armed with a spear, your advantages are also twofold. First of all, you have a great deal more range than an opponent armed with a sword; the ordinary high and low thrusts can hit a swordsman or swordswoman before he or she has a hope of hitting you, to say nothing of the long thrust, which can strike home before your opponent even realizes he or she is in danger. Your second advantage is that the spear has a great deal of momentum, and can brush aside a weakly made parry or guard as though it wasn't there at all. Your opponent will have to expend a good deal of extra energy to block your attacks, and if he or she isn't used to this, the results can favor you.

In facing the sword, keep your distance, and use quick jabbing thrusts to counter any attempt by your opponent to close in. A succession of feints and serious attacks can keep your partner on the defensive. Always try to keep your point between you and the opponent, since you are at your most vulnerable any time he or she can get past the point and close with you.

The long thrust and the combination of butt strikes and cuts are your secret weapons, and it's best not to put them to work too readily, since they leave you vulnerable. Use the long thrust when your opponent leaves himself or herself open just outside the range of your ordinary thrusts, and the combinations if he or she manages to close with you despite your efforts.

Bibliography

Historical And Theoretical Studies

Amberger, J. Christoph, *The Secret History of the Sword* (NY: 1999).
Brown, Terry, *English Martial Arts* (Hockwold-cum-Wilton, Norfolk: 1997).
Burton, Richard, *The Book of the Sword* (NY: 1987).
Castle, Egerton, *Schools and Masters of Fence* (London: 1885).
Contamine, Phillipe, *War in the Middle Ages* (Paris: 1980).
Clements, John, *Medieval Swordsmanship* (Boulder, CO: 1998).
-----, *Renaissance Swordsmanship* (Boulder, CO: 1997).
Flint, Valerie, *The Rise of Magic in Early Medieval Europe* (Princeton: 1991).
North, Anthony, *European Swords* (London: 1982).
Partner, Peter, *The Murdered Magicians: The Knights Templar and their Myth*(Oxford: 1982).
Wise, Arthur, *The Art and History of Personal Combat* (London: 1971).

Manuals Of Swordsmanship And Other Combat Arts

Berriman, Matthew W., *The Militiaman's Manual and Sword-play* (NY: 1862).
Brown, Terry, *English Martial Arts* (Hockwold-cum-Wilton, Norfolk: 1997).
Clements, John, *Medieval Swordsmanship* (Boulder, CO: 1998).
-----, *Renaissance Swordsmanship* (Boulder, CO: 1997).
Fryer, Thomas, *Short and Easy Instructions in the Broad Sword Exercise* (Carlisle: 1813).
General Staff, War Office, *Cavalry Training* (London: 1921).
Hutchinson, Fred, *The Modern Swordsman* (Boulder, CO: 1998).
Hutton, Alfred, *Old Sword-Play* (London: 1892).

Mashbir, Sidney F., *Ten Lessons In Bayonet Fighting* (Menasha, WI: 1917).

O'Rourke, Matthew J., *A New System of Sword Exercise* (NY: 1872).

Thibault, Gerard, *The Academy of the Sword*, translated by John Michael Greer (Highland Village, TX: 2005).

United States Army, *Manual of Bayonet Exercises* (Washington, D.C.: 1907).

Physical Culture Sources

"Ramacharaka, Yogi" (William Walker Atkinson), *Science of Breath* (Chicago: 1904).

Spielman, Ed, *The Spiritual Journey of Joseph L. Greenstein, The Mighty Atom* (Cobb, CA: 1998).

Stebbins, Genevieve, *Dynamic Breathing and Harmonic Gymnastics* (NY: 1893).

Index

"abdominal brain," 67
advance, 79, 125, 147, 165
basket hilt, 26, 31
bayonets, 15, 106, 109, 121, 145, 146, 161
blindfold training, 140-143
boarding pike(s), 106, 145, 161
"boffers," 32, 33
breathing exercises, 63-69, 71, 72, 78, 109, 110, 139, 148
broadsword(s), 24, 26
butt, spear, 146, 147, 148, 151-154, 157-160, 162, 165, 166
Carranza, Jeronimo, 18, 19
carry (sword position), 35, 88-89, 91, 109, 113, 118, 148
combat sword, 31, 120, 124, 126, 131, 132, 135, 149-159, 161-163, 165
Complete Breath, 65-67, 139
Cut, 24, 25, 29, 30, 31, 37, 69, 87, 89-96, 97, 100, 101, 106, 110, 111, 112, 114, 115-117, 121-125, 127-130, 133-137, 141-143, 146, 153-154, 158, 160, 162-166
cut over the guard, 131
cut under the guard, 131
diaphragm, 51, 64-67
engaging guard, 37, 100, 109, 113-115, 118, 120-121, 123, 124, 126, 131, 132, 135, 149-159, 161-163, 165
first position, 73-77, 79, 81, 87, 89-91, 113-118, 120, 121, 123-125, 129, 132, 139, 141, 148, 150, 157, 159, 161
feint, 130-131, 150, 164, 165, 166
foible, 24, 31, 69, 100, 121, 130, 131
footwork, 68, 72, 75-84, 109, 113, 118, 147, 148, 157
forte, 24, 31, 69, 100, 115, 121, 122, 130, 131
free practice, 76, 124, 125-131, 140, 164
fuller, 24
grip, (part of sword) 25, 28, 34-36, 113 (hand position) 28, 34, 69, 88-91, 96, 101, 137, 139, 147, 149, 150, 152, 159
guard, (part of sword) 25, 28, 34-35, (technique) 31, 37, 89, 100-106, 109, 110, 111, 113-124 124, 126, 128-130, 131-132, 135, 142, 149-159, 161-166
hanging guard, 37, 100, 114, 120, 122, 125, 126, 135
knights, 13-14, 17

Knights Templar, 17
knuckle bow, 25
left-handed (swordsman or swordswoman), 35-36, 72, 87, 128
line of defense, 122, 126
lodges, fraternal, 9-11, 19-20, 30
manual of the spear, 148-157
manual of the sword, 68, 86-111, 112, 125, 138, 139, 157
Marxbrüder, 14
Moulinet, 37, 106, 109, 118, 131, 162
Narvaez, Luis Pacheco de, 19
Pankration, 12
Parry, 24, 74, 98, 100-101, 107-109, 110-111, 115, 117, 118, 121, 122, 124, 128, 142, 154-159, 161-166
Pass, 80, 82, 147
physical culture, 20, 43, 133
pommel, 25, 28, 35, 36, 91
prove distance, 89, 91, 113, 150, 157, 161, 163
quarterstaff, 13, 15
quillons, 25
rapier, 18-19, 97
retreat, 79, 125-126, 147
Roman Empire, 12
saber(s)(or *sabre*), 24, 26, 31, 122
sarcofibril hypertrophy, 42
sarcoplasmotic hypertrophy, 42
schlager(s), 31
second position, 74-84, 113-114, 118, 120-121, 123, 126, 132, 148-150, 158-159
sentiment de fer, 69, 126
solar plexus, 64, 67, 68, 113, 114, 122, 126, 152, 153,
spatha, 13
spear(s), 12, 106, 109, 121, 129, 140, 144-166
step, 81
strategy, 62, 122, 126, 127-128, 164
stride, 80, 83, 129, 147, 159, 165
tang, 25, 28
Templars—see Knights Templar
Thibault, Gerard, 19
third position, 74-77, 83, 115-118, 121-124, 126, 130-131, 147, 158-159, 160, 165
three-step drills, 124
thrust, 24, 29-31, 33, 87, 89, 97-100, 106, 109-111, 112, 115-118, 121, 124-125, 127-129, 131-132, 133-137, 143, 145-147, 150-152, 158-159, 161-162, 164-166
tournaments, 13
traverse, 79-80, 125, 147
two-step drills, 123-124
visualization training, 138-140
volte, 83-84, 129, 147, 165

Other Books from The New Hermetics Press:
(discounted prices available at www.newhermetics.com)

THE BOOK OF MAGICK POWER
Jason Augustus Newcomb

This is the most comprehensive book on the subject of modern practical magick to date. Practical magick is magical work that makes real and observable changes in you and your environment through the invisible forces that manifest and transform your reality. Astral projection, telekinesis, clairvoyance, telepathy, weather magick, angelic and demonic conjuration, magnetism and fascination, manifesting love and prosperity, prophesying the future, communicating with the dead, these are just a few of the more than one hundred procedures clearly detailed in this manual. For centuries these techniques were guarded by their few masters. The veil has finally been lifted. This definitive work simply and clearly outlines the procedures necessary to open up the unseen world.

Many books on magick consist of page after page filled with philosophical and religious speculation, with just a few practical exercises of any actual use. This book takes the opposite approach, offering as much practical advice as possible and keeping philosophical discussions to a minimum. By providing a detailed plan of the exact things that one has to see, hear and feel when exploring psychic and magical phenomena- where to look, how to listen, what our internal feelings and visualizations must be, results follow simply and easily. Although this book's subject is unusual, the approach is no-nonsense and grounded in reality. Practical techniques have been broken down by step, providing an exact model for success. Unleash your limitless cosmic abilities today!

295 pages   **$24.95**

THE BROTHERHOOD OF LIGHT AND DARKNESS
a novel by Jason Augustus Newcomb

Alexander Sebastian is an armchair occult enthusiast who lacks much direction in life, but his world is turned upside down when his police detective brother-in-law asks him to help identify some magical symbols scrawled at a gruesome, ritualistic homicide. The crime is so horrific that it almost seems the killer might be some sort of demonic creature.

Alex quickly becomes obsessed with the crime, wondering who could be practicing black magick right in his hometown of Arlington, Massachusetts. He decides to find out and is quickly drawn into the underground modern magick scene. He encounters a vast array of odd characters- an obese, narcissistic, drug-peddling adept, a beautiful, coke-snorting, sex magick dominatrix, an insanely jealous Freemason who pontificates with a lisp, and many others. But is one of them a killer? Or is one of them a demonic conjurer?

To find out more, Alex joins the A.'.R.'.T.'., an international magical fraternity with a sinister reputation, discovering that the murder victim was a member of this group. He soon begins to have unusually vivid and peculiar dreams, and terrifying encounters with what appears to be the world of the supernatural. He can't tell whether these experiences are magical attacks from the killer, or just the product of his overactive imagination. As he tries to separate fact from fiction, and find out who is responsible for murder, Alex also discovers the beginning of his personal spiritual journey into the world of magical awakening.

This story is drawn largely from Newcomb's own personal experiences over the past twenty years actively participating in the modern magical community. It comes out of his real life encounters with secret magical fraternities and the unique, eccentric people that populate this sub-culture. Fans of Harry Potter or the DaVinci Code will discover what the world of magick and secret societies really looks like when you're personally involved. It reveals the world of the unknown as it truly exists, with an insider's view of the real world of Witches, Wizards, Rosicrucians and magical creatures.

308 pages, Hardcover $39.95

NEW HERMETICS EQUINOX JOURNAL VOLUME 1
edited by Jason Augustus Newcomb

This first volume of the New Hermetics Equinox Journal includes numerous updates and advancements in the New Hermetics techniques and ideas, a comparative record of several New Hermeticists conducting the "Tarot Archetype Pathworking" technique with the twenty-two trumps along with some helpful hints for students interested in greater success with this practice. This volume also includes an article on the eight seasonal holiday festivals from a New Hermetics perspective, and a collection of poetry inspired by the New Hermetics.

220 pages $21.95

NEW HERMETICS EQUINOX JOURNAL VOLUME 2
edited by Jason Augustus Newcomb

The second volume of the New Hermetics Equinox Journal contains several practical articles by Jason Augustus Newcomb on Angelic Vision Magick, Crystal Balls and Magick Mirrors, Creating Inner Harmony within the New Hermetics and the function and role of the imagination in magical practice. This volume also has a wonderful article from Philip H. Farber on creating a personal pantheon of gods as well as an extensive interview with psychedelic DMT research doctor Rick Strassman MD. Additionally, this book contains other great practical articles ranging from Alchemy to the Eight Sabbats or seasonal festivals.

200 pages $21.95

VOLUMES THREE, FOUR, FIVE AND SO ON COMING AT EACH EQUINOX!

PRACTICAL ENOCHIAN MAGICK
Jason Augustus Newcomb
Enochian Magick is arguably the most intriguing and potent form of ceremonial magick available today. Dr. John Dee, a prominent philosopher in the Elizabethan court, literally received this system of magick from angels through the scrying mediumship of Edward Kelly. Practical Enochian Magick offers a complete approach to conducting the magical system of Dr. John Dee for the modern adept. Instructions in the practical use of all three major parts of the Enochian system are contained in these pages: the Four Watchtowers, the Thirty Aethyrs and the Heptarchia Mystica. Rather than a mere rehash of Golden Dawn material this book offers an approach that honors both the innovations of the Golden Dawn and the essence of the original Dee materials in an un-dogmatic and nonsectarian format that will be extremely accessible to the New Hermetics Adept. Although this book is particularly designed for students of the New Hermetics, anyone interested in actually making use of Enochian Magick as a practicing occultist will find this book incredibly useful.
328 pages $26.95

ENOCHIAN MAGICK TOOLBOOK
Jason Augustus Newcomb
This companion volume to Practical Enochian Magick is a large format 8.5" X 11" full color book designed to help you get started conducting the rituals of Enochian Magick quickly and easily. This book contains full color prints of the four watchtowers, all of the rituals and temple openings as well as the Enochian keys on parchment scripts for use in your rituals, the talismans of the Heptarchia Mystica and other ritual accouterments to help you get started with this system of magick immediately.
132 pages $55.95

Please Visit the Newly Expanded "Products" Page at

www.newhermetics.com
or
http://shop.vendio.com/centerofchanges/

to find everything you need for practical New Hermetics magick:

- Magick Mirrors and Crystal Balls
- Ritual Candles
- New Hermetics Incense Blends
- Incense Burners, Candleholders etc.
- Tarot Decks
- Pendulums
- Statuary
- Enochian Temple Equipment
- Light & Sound Mind Machines
- Metaphysical Hypnosis CDs
- Posters and more!

Posters of the "Seven Cuts" and the "Manual of the Sword," as well as the "Ten Fundamental Exercises" are now available!

www.ingramcontent.com/pod-product-compliance
Lightning Source LLC
Chambersburg PA
CBHW032257150426
43195CB00008BA/490